mushrooms

mushrooms

Jacque Malouf

photography by Tara Fisher

 conran OCTOPUS

Soups
and Salads

Hon-shimeji, shiitake and oyster mushroom soba noodle salad

Serves 4
Preparation time: 30 minutes

2 tablespoons dried arame seaweed*
250 g/8 oz dried soba noodles
2 teaspoons sesame oil
4 teaspoons groundnut oil
100 g/3½ oz oyster mushrooms, torn into large pieces
100 g/3½ oz shiitake mushrooms, tough stalks removed, sliced
100 g/3½ oz hon-shimeji mushrooms, trimmed and separated
2 tablespoons Japanese furikake seasoning*
1 teaspoon finely shredded ginger
1 tablespoon soy sauce
1 tablespoon mirin
2 spring onions, finely sliced
1 carrot, peeled and cut into fine matchsticks
½ red chilli, deseeded and finely chopped (optional)

*available from Japanese grocers

This noodle salad is flecked with black shards of arame seaweed, lending a depth of flavour and a wonderful colour contrast. Furikake seasoning is a dry mix of seaweed, sesame and red shiso leaf.

Place the seaweed in a bowl and cover with boiling water. Leave for 5 minutes, then place in a sieve and drain well.

Boil the noodles in a pan of salted water for 4–5 minutes or until cooked. Drain and place in a bowl of cold water until cool. Drain well and place in a mixing bowl. Add the sesame oil and toss it through the noodles.

Heat the groundnut oil in a large frying pan over a high heat, then add all the mushrooms. Cook for 3 minutes or until they have coloured and softened. Set aside and allow to cool.

Add the seaweed and the cooled mushrooms to the noodles with the remaining ingredients, mix well and serve.

Sliced porcini mushrooms with lemon, parsley and olive oil

Serves 4
Preparation time: 5 minutes

200 g/7 oz small porcini mushrooms, cleaned and trimmed
2 tablespoons extra virgin olive oil
½ lemon
sea salt and freshly ground black pepper
1 tablespoon flat-leaf parsley, roughly chopped
crusty bread, to serve

This simple dish takes no time to make and has an incredible smell and nutty flavour. Although it only needs a bit of crispy bread, it works well as an antipasti dish accompanied by some Parmesan shavings and salty prosciutto.

Slice the mushrooms very finely and arrange them on a platter. Drizzle the olive oil over the mushrooms and top with a small squeeze of lemon juice. Season well, sprinkle the parsley over the mushrooms and serve with chunks of crusty bread.

When buying cultivated mushrooms, always choose fresh looking specimens with a smooth, unblemished surface. Avoid those with patches of discolouration as this can indicate deterioration. Look out for firm and dry mushrooms with a dense texture. If there is any moisture the mushrooms will be soggy and won't keep for very long. Also avoid any wrinkly ones, as they are past their prime and will yield only spongy dry flesh. For more delicate mushrooms, especially the wild varieties, choose whole, dry and unbroken mushrooms. Fuller, denser mushrooms will keep longer than finer ones that soon dry out. Avoid any mushy looking specimens as they have either been mishandled or poorly stored.

New potato, black truffle and celery heart salad

Serves 4 as a light lunch (or 6 as an accompaniment)
Preparation time: 20 minutes

500 g/1 lb small new (or waxy) potatoes, scrubbed
4 tablespoons mild olive oil
1 tablespoon white wine vinegar
30 g/1 oz (peeled weight) preserved black truffles (sold in jars), finely chopped
90 g/3 oz celery heart and/or celery leaves, washed and finely sliced
2 tablespoons chopped chives
sea salt and freshly ground black pepper
1 teaspoon of truffle oil, or to taste

This aromatic potato salad works well with grilled meats or on its own with some young salad leaves.

Cook the potatoes in a pan of boiling salted water for 10–12 minutes or until tender. Meanwhile place the oil, vinegar, truffles, celery and chives into a large bowl. Season well and add the truffle oil to taste. It is very strong, so it is best to add just a little at a time.

  Drain the potatoes, halve when they are cool enough to handle, and add to the dressing in the mixing bowl. Stir to combine and transfer to a serving bowl. Eat warm or at room temperature.

Sautéed wild mushroom salad with bacon and croûtons

Serves 4
Preparation time: 35 minutes

1 thick slice sourdough bread, cut into large cubes
1 tablespoon plus 1 teaspoon olive oil
sea salt and freshly ground black pepper
200 g/7 oz mixed wild mushrooms, brushed clean
200 g/7 oz thinly sliced streaky bacon, cut into long strips
30 g/1 oz butter
1 clove garlic, finely chopped
handful flat-leaf parsley, roughly chopped
100 g/3½ oz wild rocket (arugula)

for the dressing:
1 teaspoon seeded mustard
1 tablespoon red wine vinegar
3 tablespoons extra virgin olive oil
large pinch sugar
sea salt and freshly ground black pepper

Preheat the oven to 200°C/400°F/gas mark 6. Place the bread cubes and 1 tablespoon of olive oil in a bowl and toss to combine. Season well and place on a baking tray. Bake for 8 minutes or until crispy and golden. Set aside to cool.

  Meanwhile, place the dressing ingredients in a bowl, stir or whisk to combine and set aside.

  Keep the small mushrooms whole and tear or cut the large ones into roughly the same size. Place a frying pan over a medium to high heat and add a teaspoon of olive oil. Add the bacon and cook until crispy. Remove from the pan and set aside. Pour off any excess fat, add the butter, heat until foaming, then add the mushrooms. Cook for 2 minutes, add the garlic and cook for another 2 minutes until the mushrooms are soft and coloured. Remove from the heat, add the parsley and season well.

  Put the rocket in a large bowl and add enough dressing to coat well. Divide between 4 plates. Top with the croûtons, bacon and mushrooms and serve immediately.

Spicy glass noodle salad with enoki mushrooms, prawns and asparagus

Serves 4
Preparation time: 30 minutes

for the dressing:
1 clove garlic, finely chopped
2 tablespoons lime juice
1 tablespoon sugar
2 tablespoons Thai fish sauce*
2 tablespoons rice vinegar*
1 red chilli, deseeded and finely sliced

for the salad:
180 g/6 oz dried glass noodles*
1 teaspoon groundnut oil
120 g/4 oz fine asparagus, trimmed and woody ends
   removed
120 g/4 oz enoki mushrooms, trimmed and cut into
   individual mushrooms
180 g/6 oz cooked prawns (shrimp), peeled and deveined
2 Thai purple shallots, peeled and finely sliced*
30 g/1 oz roasted, unsalted peanuts, chopped
small handful coriander (cilantro) leaves
small handful Thai basil leaves*
small handful mint leaves

*available from Oriental grocers

Although not burn-your-mouth hot, this spicy salad should have a bit of a kick. You can add more or less chilli depending on your tolerance. The recipe works just as well with shredded cooked chicken in place of the prawns.

Glass noodles, also called cellophane noodles, are made from mung beans. Available from Oriental grocers, they are sometimes sold as mung bean thread noodles.

Make the dressing by placing the ingredients in a bowl and stirring to combine. Set aside while you prepare the salad.

Soak the noodles in boiling water for 5 minutes, then tip into a colander and transfer to a bowl of cold water. Drain again, shake well and place in a large bowl. Cut the noodles into smaller lengths with kitchen scissors. Add the groundnut oil and stir through the noodles to prevent them sticking.

Place the asparagus in a pan of boiling salted water for 1 minute. Drain in a colander, place in a bowl of cold water to cool and drain again. Add the asparagus to the noodles with the rest of the salad ingredients. Add most of the dressing and taste, adding the rest if necessary. Toss to combine, and serve.

Olive oil braised baby button mushrooms

Makes about 250 g/8 oz drained mushrooms plus extra oil for dipping
Preparation time: 1 hour 15 minutes

300 g/10 oz baby button mushrooms, wiped clean
2 bay leaves
2 cloves garlic, peeled and lightly crushed
4 sprigs thyme
4 wide strips lemon peel, pith removed
½ teaspoon sea salt flakes
½ teaspoon whole black peppercorns
140 ml/¼ pint olive oil

These tasty mushrooms and their braising oil take on the bold flavours of the garlic, thyme and lemon, making them perfect for mopping up with crusty bread. Try them with other marinated vegetables, such as sun-dried tomatoes and grilled artichokes.

Preheat the oven to 150°C/300°F/gas mark 2. Place the mushrooms in a single layer in a cast iron roasting tin or casserole. Scatter over the bay leaves, garlic, thyme, lemon peel, salt and pepper. Pour the olive oil over the mushrooms and stir to coat them well.

Cover tightly with foil and place in the oven for an hour. Remove from the oven and allow to cool. Serve with lots of crusty bread for dunking in the infused oil.

Grilled vegetables with anchovies, Niçoise olives and basil

Serves 4 (or 6 as an accompaniment)
Preparation time: 1 hour

2 large portabello mushrooms, thickly sliced
1 medium courgette (zucchini), trimmed and cut lengthways into thin slices
1 large romano pepper, deseeded and cut into large strips
1 small red onion, peeled and cut into 8 wedges
1 small aubergine, trimmed and cut into thick slices
6 tablespoons extra virgin olive oil
salt and freshly ground black pepper
1 tablespoon aged balsamic vinegar
60 g/2 oz Niçoise olives in oil (or any good quality small black olives), pitted
8 Spanish anchovies in olive oil, cut in half lengthways
a handful basil leaves
crusty bread, to serve

Preheat a large cast iron chargrill over a very high heat. Alternatively, you can use a barbecue. Put the mushrooms, courgette, pepper, onion and aubergine into a large bowl with 2 tablespoons of the oil and some freshly ground black pepper. Toss until the vegetables are evenly coated. Grill the vegetables in batches, preferably using just 1 or 2 varieties at a time as the cooking times will vary. Grill on both sides until cooked through and tender. When all the vegetables are cooked, transfer them to a large wide bowl.

Whisk the remaining oil with the balsamic vinegar. Finely chop half each of the olives, anchovies and basil and stir through the dressing. Add some pepper, and a small amount of salt only if it needs it, as anchovies can be very salty. Pour the dressing over the vegetables with the remaining olives and anchovies and stir to coat well. Transfer to a large serving platter and scatter over the remaining basil leaves. Serve with chunks of crusty bread and eat slightly warm or at room temperature.

Pork, prawn and dried cloud ear wonton soup

Serves 4
Preparation time: 50 minutes, plus 3 hours to make the stock

for the broth (makes 2–2½ litres/about 3½–4 pints):
900 g/2 lb chicken bones
450 g/1 lb pork ribs, separated
4 spring onions, cleaned and cut into 4
15 g/½ oz ginger, peeled and sliced
2 tablespoons Chinese rice wine*
2 tablespoons soy sauce

for the wontons:
2 dried cloud ears (also known as black fungus)*
120 g/4 oz minced pork
60 g/2 oz raw prawns (shrimp), peeled, cleaned and
    chopped
1 spring onion, finely chopped
1 teaspoon ginger, finely chopped
2 teaspoons soy sauce
1 teaspoon caster sugar
½ teaspoon sesame oil
2 teaspoons Chinese rice wine*
pinch ground white pepper
24 wonton skins*

for the soup:
½ quantity Chinese broth (see above)
extra soy sauce (optional)
3 spring onions, finely chopped

* available from Oriental grocers

The broth will make enough for two wonton soup recipes, as it's not worth the bother of making a small amount of stock. You can freeze the second half for later use. The rich fragrant broth always comes in handy in Chinese recipes.

If you don't want to make the broth, the wontons work just as well on their own. For a tasty party snack, try deep-frying the raw wontons and serving with some sweet chilli sauce for dipping.

To make the broth, rinse the chicken bones and pork ribs and place them in a large saucepan. Add the spring onions and ginger and top with 3½ litres/6 pints of cold water. Place over a high heat and bring to the boil. Remove any scum that has risen to the surface, turn down to a simmer and cook for 2½ hours, regularly skimming off any fat and scum that float to the surface. Add the rice wine and soy sauce and cook for a further 10 minutes. Strain the broth through muslin or a fine sieve into a bowl.

To make the wonton filling, place the dried cloud ears in a bowl and cover with boiling water. Leave to soften for 10 minutes. Strain and allow to cool before finely chopping. Place in a large bowl with the rest of the filling ingredients and mix until well combined. Place a wonton skin on a flat surface, covering the rest until they are needed as they tend to dry out. Using a pastry brush, moisten the four edges with some water and place a heaped teaspoon of the filling in the middle. Fold over diagonally to form a triangle and seal by pressing down along the moistened edges. Moisten the two corners along the folded edge and bring them to the front, pinching them together to seal. Place on a large plate or tray and continue until you have 24 wontons. Do not crowd the plate, as they can stick together.

When ready to serve, place the broth into a large pot and bring up to a simmer. Add the wontons, one at a time so they don't stick together. Cook for 4 minutes, stirring occasionally. It may be easier to cook them in two batches if your pan isn't very big. Taste the broth and season with soy sauce if required. Divide between four soup bowls and garnish with the chopped spring onions.

Creamy wild mushroom soup with truffle oil and Parmesan crostini

Serves 4
Preparation time: 1 hour 15 minutes

for the Parmesan crostini:
12 thin slices baguette, sliced diagonally
1 clove garlic, peeled
2 teaspoons olive oil
30 g/1 oz Parmesan cheese, grated
salt and freshly ground black pepper

for the soup:
30 g/1 oz butter
1 onion, finely chopped
1 small clove garlic, finely chopped
260 g/8½ oz wild mushrooms, cleaned and torn or cut into
    small pieces
180 g/6 oz cultivated mushrooms, sliced
800 ml/1½ pints chicken stock
140 ml/5 oz whipping cream
truffle oil
salt and freshly ground black pepper

To make the crostini, preheat the oven to 180°C/350°F/gas mark 4. Place the baguette slices on a baking tray and rub with the garlic clove. Brush with the oil and scatter over the Parmesan. Season and place in the oven for 10 minutes. Serve warm or at room temperature with the soup.

To make the soup, place the butter in a saucepan over a medium heat. Add the onion and garlic and cook until soft. Add all the mushrooms and cook for a further 6–7 minutes or until they are soft. Pour in the stock, bring up to a gentle simmer and cook for 20 minutes. Transfer to a blender or food processor (you will need to do this in batches) and whizz until smooth. Place the puréed soup back into the pan and add the cream. Season and add a few drops of truffle oil (it is very powerful). Taste and adjust the seasoning. Serve in four warm soup bowls and hand round the crostini.

Shiitake mushroom miso soup

Serves 4
Preparation time: 20 minutes

for the dashi (basic Japanese soup stock):
15 cm/6 in square piece dried kombu
15 g/½ oz dried bonito flakes

for the miso soup:
2 tablespoons miso paste
8 shiitake mushrooms, tough stalks removed, finely sliced
120 g/4 oz firm tofu, cubed
1 small spring onion, finely sliced

Kombu is salted dried kelp that is used in many Japanese soups and stocks. Bonito flakes are shavings of dried fish used in stocks and as a condiment. Miso paste is a fermented soy bean paste used as a flavouring for many Japanese recipes. All are available from Japanese grocers.

To make the dashi, place the kombu in a saucepan with 1 litre (1¾ pints) cold water. Place over a high heat and bring to the boil. Turn off the heat and sprinkle in the bonito flakes. Leave for 3 minutes then strain through a fine sieve.

To make the miso soup, place all but 100ml of the strained dashi into a saucepan over a medium heat and bring to a simmer. Add the miso paste to the reserved dashi, stir or whisk until combined and add it to the pan. Add the sliced mushrooms and cook for 3 minutes. Place the tofu and spring onions into four small warm bowls. Pour over the hot miso soup and serve straight away.

Porcini mushroom, spinach and lentil broth with lemon, garlic and olive oil

Serves 4
Preparation time: 40 minutes

2 cloves garlic, roughly chopped
sea salt and freshly ground black pepper
900 ml/1½ pints well-seasoned chicken stock
90 g/3½ oz green lentils
150 g/5 oz new potatoes, peeled, cubed and placed in a
    bowl of water
20 g/⅔ oz dried porcini mushrooms
150 g/5 oz spinach leaves, washed and roughly chopped
3 tablespoons lemon juice
6 tablespoons extra virgin olive oil

Pound the garlic with half a teaspoon of sea salt in a mortar and pestle until you have a smooth paste and set aside.

Place the stock, lentils and potatoes into a saucepan and bring up to the boil, skimming regularly to remove any foamy residue from the surface. Lower the heat slightly and cook for 20 minutes, or until the lentils and potatoes are tender. While they are cooking, soak the mushrooms in 250ml (8 fl oz) of warm water for 15 minutes to soften. Squeeze the mushrooms dry and set aside in a bowl. Strain the mushroom water through a fine sieve and return it to the mushrooms. Once the lentils and potatoes are soft, add the reserved mushrooms and their water. Add the spinach leaves and cook for 1 minute or until tender. Add the pounded garlic, lemon juice and olive oil and cook for a further minute. Turn off the heat, taste and season well. Pour into four warm bowls and eat with lots of crusty bread.

Thai chicken, coconut and hon-shimeji mushroom soup

Serves 4
Preparation time: 20 minutes

480 ml/16 fl oz chicken stock
720 ml/1 pint 4 fl oz coconut milk
2 stalks lemongrass, cut into lengths and crushed*
6 lime leaves, torn*
1 red chilli, deseeded and roughly chopped
1 2½ cm/1 inch piece galangal (Thai ginger), peeled and cut
    into 6 slices*
1 teaspoon finely chopped coriander stalks, taken from the
    root end
120 g/4 oz hon-shimeji mushrooms, separated and
    trimmed
180 g/6 oz free range or organic chicken breast, finely
    sliced
½ teaspoon sugar
2 tablespoons Thai fish sauce (nam pla)*
2 tablespoons lime juice, plus extra for seasoning
small handful coriander leaves
1 red chilli, deseeded and finely sliced
* available from Oriental grocers

This deliciously perfumed Thai soup, known as Tom Kha Gai, is full of fresh flavours. The galangal, lime leaves and lemongrass are there to infuse the coconut milk and, although fine to eat, are best avoided as they can be tough and woody.

Place the chicken stock and coconut milk in a saucepan with the lemongrass, lime leaves, chilli, galangal and coriander root. Bring up to a gentle simmer and add the mushrooms and chicken. Cook for 4 minutes and season with the sugar, fish sauce and lime juice. Taste and add more lime juice if it is needed. Transfer to four warm bowls, garnish with the coriander leaves and sliced chilli and serve.

Pasta, Couscous and Rice

Spaghetti with crimini mushrooms, pancetta, chilli and garlic

Serves 4
Preparation time: 20 minutes

360 g/12 oz dried spaghetti
100 g/3½ oz smoked pancetta, thinly sliced
3 tablespoons olive oil
200 g/7 oz crimini mushrooms, thinly sliced
1 large clove garlic, finely chopped
1 red chilli, deseeded and finely chopped
sea salt and freshly ground black pepper
handful flat-leaf parsley, roughly chopped
60 g/2 oz Parmesan cheese, grated (optional)

Cook the spaghetti in a large pan of boiling salted water.

While the spaghetti is cooking, place the pancetta in a large sauté pan over a medium to high heat. Cook for 4 minutes or until crispy, then remove with a slotted spoon and set aside. Add 2 tablespoons of olive oil to the pan and add the mushrooms. Cook for 2 minutes, then add the garlic and chilli and cook for a further 3–4 minutes. Add the cooked pancetta, season well and take off the heat.

Drain the pasta, reserving 2 tablespoons of the cooking water to moisten the sauce. Add the spaghetti to the mushrooms and pancetta. Add the reserved water from the pasta, the remaining olive oil and the chopped parsley. Stir to combine, sprinkle over the cheese (if using) and serve straight away.

Pappardelle with sausage, wild mushroom and tomato ragout

Serves 4
Preparation time: 1 hour 30 minutes

20 g/⅔ oz dried wild mushrooms (try porcini or morels)
1 tablespoon olive oil
1 onion, finely chopped
1 clove garlic, finely chopped
280 g/9 oz free-range sausages, skinned
pinch dried chilli flakes
60 ml/2 fl oz white wine
2 sprigs thyme
1 bay leaf
400 g/13 oz tin chopped Italian plum tomatoes
salt and freshly ground black pepper
300 g/10½ oz dried egg pappardelle pasta
handful flat-leaf parsley, roughly chopped
grated Parmesan cheese, to serve

Place the dried mushrooms in a bowl and cover with warm water. Leave to soften for 20 minutes, then remove and squeeze dry. Set the mushrooms aside and reserve the mushroom water separately.

Place the olive oil in a pan over a medium heat. Add the onion and garlic and cook for 7 minutes or until they soften. Tip into a bowl and wipe out the pan. Place it back on the heat and add the sausage meat. Break up the meat with a fork and cook for 10 minutes or until it colours. Add the chilli flakes, wine, thyme, bay leaf, mushrooms and softened onions and cook until any liquid evaporates. Add the tomatoes and cook until they bubble briskly. Lower the heat and cook for 45 minutes, bubbling gently. Add a small amount of the reserved mushroom water if the sauce becomes dry during cooking. Take off the heat, season well and cover until needed.

Meanwhile, cook the pasta until al dente in a large pan of boiling salted water. Drain well, return to the pan and stir through the sauce. Add a little more mushroom water if it needs it. Stir in the parsley and serve with grated Parmesan.

Buttered tagliolini with white truffles

Serves 2
Preparation time: 10 minutes

150 g/5 oz dried tagliolini pasta
45 g/1½ oz butter, cubed
1 fresh white truffle, about the size of a large shallot,
  brushed clean
salt and freshly ground black pepper

The heady perfume of the fresh white truffle combined with its extortionate price makes this luxurious pasta a very rare treat. Serve as often as you can afford and enjoy!

Place the pasta in a pan of boiling salted water and cook until al dente. Drain into a colander and put back into the pan with the butter. Shave over half the truffle, using a truffle slicer or mandolin. Stir to combine, lightly season and serve on two warm plates. Shave the rest of the truffle over the pasta and serve immediately.

Wild mushroom open lasagne

Serves 4 as a starter
Preparation time: 45 minutes

for the pesto:
30 g/1 oz basil leaves
2 heaped tablespoons pine nuts, toasted
30 g/1 oz pecorino cheese, grated
1 small clove garlic, roughly chopped
3 tablespoons olive oil

200 g/7 oz mixed wild mushrooms, cleaned
30 g/1 oz butter
4 tablespoons white wine
150 ml/5 fl oz double cream
sea salt and freshly ground black pepper
60 g/2 oz pecorino cheese, grated
8 fresh lasagne sheets
1 tablespoon olive oil
2 heaped tablespoons pine nuts, toasted

Whizz the pesto ingredients in a food processor or blender until they form a smooth paste. Place in a bowl and set aside.

Tear or slice the mushrooms into even-sized pieces. Small mushrooms can be kept whole. Melt the butter in a frying pan over a medium to high heat and add the mushrooms. Fry briskly for 5 minutes until evenly coloured. Add the wine and cook until it evaporates. Add 2 tablespoons of cream, season, then take off the heat and keep warm until needed.

Place the remaining cream in a small pan over a low heat. Add the pesto and stir until warmed through. Add half of the cheese and stir to combine, then set aside and keep warm.

Bring a large pan of salted water to the boil, remove from the heat and drop in the lasagne sheets. Leave for 5 minutes then drain. Put the pasta back in the pan with the olive oil and stir gently to prevent them sticking together. For each serving, lay a pasta sheet on every plate, cover with a tablespoon of mushrooms, then a heaped tablespoon of pesto cream. Add a second layer of all three, then scatter with pine nuts and the remaining pecorino. Serve immediately.

Baked gnocchi with sautéed trompettes de mort and pied bleu mushrooms in a gorgonzola cream sauce

Serves 4
Preparation time: 1 hour, plus 40 minutes to steam the potatoes

450 g/15 oz Desirée potatoes (roughly the same size)
90 g/3 oz plain flour
1½ teaspoons fine sea salt
150 ml/5 oz single cream
150 g/5 oz gorgonzola cheese, cut into small cubes
sea salt and freshly ground black pepper
15 g/½ oz butter
200 g/7 oz mixture of trompettes de mort and pied bleu mushrooms, cleaned and torn or cut into even pieces

These light-as-a-feather gnocchi can be cooked a few hours in advance, covered with the sauce and mushrooms, and then baked at the last minute. Alternatively, they can be served as loose pasta, with the gnocchi simply tossed with the sauce and mushrooms and served piping hot. If you have any difficulty obtaining them, the trompettes de mort and pied bleu mushrooms can be substituted with other wild mushrooms.

Make the gnocchi by steaming the potatoes in their skins for 40 minutes or until tender. Using rubber gloves and a small knife, peel the hot potatoes and mash them using a potato ricer or mouli-legumes. Tip out on to a lightly floured work surface and sprinkle the flour and salt over the top. Knead with your hands until the flour is incorporated and the dough is nice and smooth.

Divide the dough in half and lightly flour the work surface. Take one of the pieces of dough and roll, using your fingers, into a long 2 cm/¾ in wide sausage. Cut the sausage into 2cm/¾ in pieces and place them on a lightly floured board. Repeat with the rest of the dough. Gently flatten and make an imprint into each piece using the prongs of a fork. Cover and set aside.

Put the cream into a small saucepan set over a medium heat and bring up to a gentle bubble. Lower the heat and add the cheese. Stir until the cheese is combined and season to taste. Take off the heat and set aside until needed.

Melt the butter in a large frying pan placed over a high heat. Add the mushrooms and fry briskly for 2 minutes or until soft. Season well, transfer to a bowl and set aside.

Preheat the oven to 200°C/400°F/gas mark 6. Bring a large pot of boiling salted water to a simmer and tip in half the gnocchi. Cook for 2–3 minutes or until they bob up to the surface of the water. Remove with a slotted spoon and place on absorbent kitchen paper. Cook the rest of the gnocchi, drain on the kitchen paper and allow to cool slightly. Gently tip the gnocchi into a mixing bowl. Spoon half of the cheese sauce over the gnocchi and stir well to coat each piece. Tip into a buttered ovenproof dish and scatter the mushrooms over the top. Pour the remaining sauce on top, place in the oven for 20 minutes or until the sauce is bubbling and serve at once.

Mixed mushroom, prosciutto and ricotta rotolo

Serves 4–6
Preparation time: 2 hours 40 minutes

for the pasta dough:
185 g/6½ oz plain flour, plus extra flour for dusting
large pinch fine sea salt
2 large eggs

for the filling:
60 g/2 oz butter
2 cloves garlic, finely chopped
600 g/1 lb 3 oz mixed wild and/or cultivated mushrooms,
    cleaned and torn or cut into even-sized pieces
250 g/9 oz ricotta cheese
75 g/3 oz pecorino cheese, grated
6 large slices prosciutto

for the cheese sauce:
30 g/1 oz butter
1 level tablespoon plain flour
250 ml/8 fl oz milk, warmed
30 g/1 oz pecorino cheese, grated
a few fresh grindings of nutmeg
sea salt and freshly ground black pepper

for the top:
30 g/1 oz pecorino cheese, grated

To make the pasta dough, sift the flour and salt on to a work surface and create a well in the middle. Break the eggs into the well. Using your fingers and working from the centre out, mix the eggs into the flour to make a thick paste. Lightly flour the board and knead with the heel of your hand for 10 minutes or until the dough is smooth and elastic. Cover with clingfilm and leave to rest for an hour.

To make the filling, melt the butter in a large saucepan over a medium heat. Add the garlic, cook for a minute, then add the mushrooms and cook for 10 minutes or until they soften and the liquid evaporates. Place in a large mixing bowl to cool. Once cooled, stir in the cheeses and season well.

To make the cheese sauce, melt the butter in a small pan over a medium heat. Add the flour and stir or whisk until smooth. Cook for 1 minute, stirring often. Add a splash of the warm milk and stir until smooth. Gradually add the rest of the milk in small amounts, stirring well between batches. Add the cheese once it begins to thicken, and stir until smooth and thick. Season with the nutmeg, salt and pepper. Transfer to a bowl, cover with clingfilm and set aside.

To make the rotolo, place a clean tea towel on a large work surface or board. Place the dough on a floured work surface. Using a rolling pin, roll the pasta very thinly and large enough to cut out a 30 x 40 cm/12 x 16 in rectangle. Transfer the pasta to a clean tea towel and cover with clingfilm.

Fill a fish kettle or very large stockpot with salted water, place over a high heat and bring to the boil. Meanwhile, remove the clingfilm from the pasta sheet and cover with the prosciutto slices, leaving a 2½ cm/1 in border around the edge. Evenly cover the prosciutto with the mushroom and ricotta mixture. Lift one of the longer lengths of the tea towel and roll up the pasta like a Swiss roll, squeezing firmly as you go to compress the roll. Tightly tie the ends with some string. You should have an even, firm parcel inside a tightly tied tea towel.

Gently slide the pasta roll into the boiling salted water. If the pan isn't wide enough, carefully coil the pasta roll along the inside of the pan. Cook for 20 minutes at a gentle boil. Carefully remove from the water and transfer to a board. Once cool enough to handle, gently remove the tea towel and allow the roll to cool (if it cools while wrapped in the tea towel it will stick to it). Don't worry if there are slight cracks in the pasta, as these can occur if the roll is curved in the pan.

Preheat the oven to 200°C/400°F/gas mark 5. Lightly butter a 20 x 30cm/8 x 12in baking dish and set aside. Once the pasta roll is completely cool, slice off the 2 ends so you have an even log with no tapering at the edges. Discard the ends and cut the roll into 16 slices. Arrange the slices in the buttered dish so they slightly overlap. Pour the cheese sauce over the top and sprinkle with the cheese. Place in the oven for 20 minutes or until golden and bubbling. Let the pasta sit for a few minutes, then serve it in its dish.

Porcini mushroom risotto

Serves 4
Preparation time: 1 hour

45 g/1¾ oz dried porcini mushrooms
1 litre/1¾ pints well-seasoned chicken stock
2 tablespoons olive oil
1 onion, finely chopped
330 g/11 oz arborio rice
100 ml/3½ fl oz dry white wine
75 g/2½ oz butter, cubed
90 g/3½ oz freshly grated Parmesan cheese
salt and freshly ground black pepper
truffle oil, to serve (optional)

If you intend to use this recipe as a base for Porcini
Mushroom Risotto Balls (page 91), use a little less
stock as the risotto shouldn't be too wet.

Put the mushrooms in a bowl, cover with 300 ml (½ pint)
warm water and leave to soften for 20 minutes. Squeeze
them dry, then roughly chop and set aside until needed.
Strain the mushroom water through muslin or a fine sieve
into a large saucepan. Add the stock and heat to a gentle
simmer. Keep over a low heat while you prepare the risotto.

Pour the olive oil into a large heavy-based pan set over a
medium to low heat. Add the onion and cook for 6 minutes
or until completely soft but not coloured. Turn up the heat
and stir in the rice. Cook and stir for a minute, then add the
wine and let it sizzle and evaporate. Add the mushrooms and
a ladleful of the hot stock to the pan and stir until it is
almost all absorbed. Continue ladle by ladle until most of the
stock is absorbed and the rice is cooked but maintains a firm
bite. This will take about 20 minutes. Turn down the heat if
it bubbles too much or begins to stick to the pan. Add some
of the remaining stock and stir until you have a wet, but not
sloppy, risotto. Don't worry if there is a little leftover stock.

Turn off the heat and stir in the butter and Parmesan.
Cover for a few minutes, taste and season. Add a few drops
of truffle oil if you are using it and serve.

Spicy shiitake and oyster mushroom fried rice

Serves 2–3
Preparation time: 15 minutes

3 tablespoons groundnut oil
1 clove garlic, chopped
90 g/3½ oz shiitake mushrooms, tough stems removed and
  caps sliced
90 g/3½ oz oyster mushrooms, torn into pieces
60 g/2½ oz frozen peas, defrosted
2 spring onions, finely sliced
2 large eggs, lightly beaten
450 g/15 oz cooked basmati rice, cooled
2 tablespoons Thai thin soy sauce*
1 teaspoon hot chilli sauce* (or more if you can handle it!)
½ teaspoon sugar
1 teaspoon sesame oil

* available from Oriental grocers

Place the oil in a large wok placed over a high heat. Add the
garlic, mushrooms and peas and cook for 1 minute. Add the
spring onions and eggs and cook for a further minute,
stirring well to scramble the eggs. Add the rice and cook for
3 minutes until piping hot, tossing well to distribute the
heat. Season with the soy sauce, chilli sauce, sugar and
sesame oil. Remove from the heat and serve straight away.

Cinnamon-spiced couscous, button mushroom and minced lamb salad with pistachio nuts and cumin yoghurt dressing

Serves 4, or 6 as part of a buffet
Preparation time: 40 minutes

for the yoghurt dressing:
150 g/5 oz natural yoghurt
½ teaspoon cumin
1 tablespoon lemon juice
salt and freshly ground black pepper

175 g/6 oz couscous
3 tablespoons olive oil
250 ml/8 fl oz hot chicken stock
1 red onion, chopped
250 g/8 fl oz minced lamb
200 g/7 oz button mushrooms, sliced
½ teaspoon sugar
1 teaspoon ground cinnamon
1 teaspoon ground coriander
1 teaspoon ground cumin
150 g/5 oz tinned chickpeas, drained
45 g/2 oz pistachio nuts, chopped
5 tablespoons roughly chopped flat-leaf parsley
5 tablespoons roughly chopped mint leaves
1 tablespoon lemon juice
salt and freshly ground black pepper

This Lebanese-inspired dish can be served warm or at room temperature, making it a great addition to a Middle Eastern mezze-style buffet. Try it with toasted Lebanese bread and grilled courgettes if it is to be eaten as a separate meal.

Make the dressing by mixing the ingredients together and seasoning well. Set aside until needed.

Place the couscous in a large mixing bowl and cover with a tablespoon of olive oil. Stir well to coat each grain and pour over the hot stock. Stir, then cover for 10 minutes or until soft. Use a fork to separate the grains, season and set aside.

Place a large non-stick frying pan over a medium heat and add the remaining olive oil. Add the chopped onion and cook for 2 minutes or until softened. Transfer to a bowl, then turn up the heat and add the lamb to the pan. Break up the meat with a wooden spoon and cook for 4 minutes or until it browns. Add the mushrooms and cook for a further 2 minutes or until they soften. Return the cooked onions, add the sugar, cinnamon, coriander and cumin, season well and cook for a further minute. Remove from the heat and tip into the bowl with the couscous. Add the chickpeas, pistachio nuts, herbs and lemon juice, mix well and season to taste. Transfer to a serving platter and top with the yoghurt dressing.

Pies, Pastry, Tarts and Breads

Mixed mushroom, spinach and Parmesan tart

Serves 6–8
Preparation time: 1 hour, plus 1 hour 30 minutes to make the pastry

2 tablespoons olive oil
30 g/1 oz butter
450 g/1 lb cultivated mushrooms (try crimini, button or portabello), sliced
1½ teaspoons thyme leaves, chopped
350 g/12 oz tender spinach leaves, washed and drained
2 large eggs
200 ml/7 oz double cream
100 g/3½ oz Parmesan cheese, grated
salt and freshly ground black pepper
1 x 25 cm (10 in) prepared tart case (using the parmesan shortcrust pastry recipe, right)

Place the olive oil and butter in a large saucepan over a medium heat. Add the mushrooms and thyme and cook for 15 minutes, stirring regularly, until any liquid evaporates. Tip into a bowl.

Place the pan over a high heat. Put the spinach into the pan and cook until soft and wilted. Transfer the cooked spinach to a colander. Press down with a wooden spoon to remove any excess moisture. Transfer to a plate to cool.

Preheat the oven to 180°C/350°F/gas mark 4. Using your hands, squeeze the excess moisture out of the cooked spinach. Roughly chop, then add to the cooked mushrooms and season well. Place the eggs and double cream in a bowl and whisk to combine. Add the Parmesan, season well and stir. Spread the spinach and mushroom mixture over the prepared tart base and pour over the creamy liquid. Place in the oven and cook for 25 minutes. Take out and allow to stand for at least 10 minutes before removing from the tin. Eat hot, warm or at room temperature.

Parmesan shortcrust pastry

Lines 1 tart case for a 4 cm/
1½ inch deep 25 cm/10 in tart tin
Preparation time: 1 hour 30 minutes

175 g/6 oz plain flour, plus extra for dusting
75 g/3 oz cold butter, cubed
45 g/1¾ oz parmesan cheese, finely grated
1 large egg yolk
2½ tablespoons cold water
freshly ground black pepper

Place the flour and butter in a food processor or mixer and whiz until it resembles fine breadcrumbs. Add the Parmesan, egg yolk, cold water and a few grindings of black pepper and whizz briefly until the mixture comes together, adding a tiny bit more water if necessary. Place on a work surface and lightly gather with your hands, working it into a rough ball. Flatten lightly to form a large disc, cover with clingfilm and refrigerate for at least 45 minutes (the chosen tart filling can be prepared during this time).

Preheat the oven to 180°C/350°F/gas mark 4. Take the pastry out of the fridge and bring up to room temperature before attempting to roll it. Roll the pastry into a 35 cm/14 in disc on a lightly floured surface. Gently transfer to a 25 cm/10 in loose-bottomed tart tin with 4 cm/1½ in high sides. The easiest way to do this is to roll the pastry around a floured rolling pin and drape it over the tin. Carefully press it into place and prick the base with a fork. Place a large sheet of baking parchment over the pastry case and fill with baking beans. Place on a tray and transfer to the oven. Cook for 15 minutes then take out and remove the baking beans and parchment. Return to the oven for a further 10 minutes to crisp up the base. Remove from the oven and allow to cool slightly. Use a small knife to trim any excess pastry from around the rim. The tart case is now ready to be filled.

Chicken, mushroom and leek cobbler

Serves 6
Preparation time: 1 hour 30 minutes

for the filling:
4 tablespoons olive oil
175 g/6 oz closed-cap mushrooms, cleaned and quartered
1 large leek, washed and finely sliced
4 tablespoons plain flour, seasoned
750 g/1½ lb free range or organic chicken thighs, skin and bones removed
150 ml/5 fl oz white wine
200 ml/7 fl oz chicken stock
150 ml/5 fl oz double cream
1 tablespoon chopped tarragon
sea salt and freshly ground black pepper

for the scone dough:
175 g/6 oz self-raising flour, plus extra for dusting
90 g/3½ oz Cheddar cheese, grated
sea salt and freshly ground black pepper
150 ml/5 fl oz milk, plus extra for brushing

This moreish cobbler consists of a rich chicken and mushroom filling topped with a cheesy scone dough. Serve with some buttered beans or spinach for a winter supper or a green salad for a lighter meal.

To make the filling, place a tablespoon of the oil into a large sauté pan placed over a medium high heat. Add the mushrooms and cook for 1–2 minutes or until lightly browned. Remove from the heat and transfer to a plate. Add another tablespoon of the oil and cook the leek for 1–2 minutes or until lightly browned. Take off the heat and add the leek to the mushrooms.

Place half the flour in a mixing bowl and add the chicken. Toss well to coat each piece and shake to remove any excess flour. Add the remaining oil to the sauté pan and set over a high heat. Add the chicken and cook for 4 minutes on each side or until nicely browned. Sprinkle over the flour left in the bowl and cook for a further minute. Pour in the wine and cook for another minute, stirring until smooth. Add the stock and bring up to a simmer, scraping the base of the pan with a wooden spoon to incorporate the sticky bits. Turn down the heat to maintain a gentle simmer, cover and cook for 20 minutes. Remove from the heat and tear the chicken into large chunks using two forks. Add the mushrooms, leeks, cream and tarragon and stir to combine. Taste and season well, then tip into a large ovenproof pie or baking dish that will comfortably hold the filling. Preheat the oven to 190°C/375°F/gas mark 5.

To make the scone dough, place the flour in a large mixing bowl and add the cheese. Season very well and slowly add the milk, mixing the dough with a knife until it comes together into a rough ball. Turn out on to a well-floured board and roll into a piece that will fit the top of the pie dish.

Place the rolled dough so that it covers the filling and then lightly brush with milk. Transfer to a baking sheet and bake for 20–25 minutes or until the cobbler topping is golden and risen.

Portabello mushroom, lemon thyme and goat's cheese flan

Serves 4
Preparation time: 50 minutes

8 medium portabello mushrooms
sea salt and freshly ground black pepper
1 clove garlic, finely sliced
2 teaspoons chopped lemon thyme leaves
2 tablespoons olive oil
flour for rolling the pastry
375 g/12 oz packet of puff pastry
1 egg, lightly beaten
finely grated zest of 1 lemon
200 g/7 oz soft rindless goat's cheese
1 tablespoon chopped flat-leaf parsley
fine strips of lemon zest, to serve

These tasty, easy flans can also be prepared as four individual portions. Just cut each pastry length in half, score the inside edges and cover with the toppings.

Serve with some spicy salad leaves, such as rocket (arugula) or watercress and an olive oil dressing with the merest hint of aged vinegar or lemon juice.

Preheat the oven to 220°C/425°F/gas mark 7. Place the mushrooms gill side up on a lightly oiled roasting tin and season well. Scatter the garlic slices and half the thyme over the mushroom gills and drizzle with the oil. Place in the oven and cook for 10 minutes. Set aside and allow to cool.

Meanwhile, lightly flour a work surface and roll the puff pastry into a 36 x 22 cm/14 x 9 in rectangle. Some brands of puff pastry are sold in sheets of these dimensions. Cut the pastry in half lengthways so you have two long rectangles. Score a 1 cm/½ in border inside the edge of each piece, using a small sharp knife. Place the two pieces of pastry on a large lightly oiled baking tray and brush each border with the beaten egg. Mix the lemon zest with the goat's cheese and smear it within the border. Arrange the mushrooms on top and sprinkle over the remaining thyme. Season, then place in the oven for 15 minutes. Remove from the oven and allow to cool slightly. Scatter the parsley and lemon zest over the top and serve.

Crimini mushroom, pancetta and red onion tart

Serves 6–8
Preparation time: 1 hour, plus 1 hour 30 minutes to make the pastry base

2 tablespoons olive oil
200 g/7 oz pancetta, thinly sliced
1 large red onion, peeled and sliced
sea salt and freshly ground black pepper
250 g/8 oz crimini mushrooms, cleaned
150 g/5 oz crème fraîche
150 ml/5 fl oz double cream
1 large egg plus 1 yolk
1 x 25 cm/10 in prepared tart case (using the Parmesan short crust pastry recipe, page 34)

This gooey tart is fabulously rich and creamy. The mild tang of the crème fraîche is a perfect match for the sweet red onion and salty pancetta. You can use button or chestnut mushrooms instead of crimini if they are easier to come by.

Place a tablespoon of the oil in a frying pan set over a medium heat. Add the pancetta and cook for 3 minutes or until it begins to colour. Add the onions to the pan and cook for a further 3–4 minutes or until they soften. Season well, then remove from the pan and transfer to a bowl to cool. Place the remaining oil in the pan and add the mushrooms. Stir to coat in the oil, cover, then lower the heat and cook for 10 minutes or until the mushrooms are tender. Transfer to a plate and set aside to cool.

Preheat the oven to 180°C/350°F/gas mark 4. Whisk the crème fraîche, double cream and eggs together and season well. Scatter the pancetta and onions over the baked tart base. Arrange the mushrooms over the top in a neat single layer. Pour the creamy mixture over the mushrooms and place in the oven for 30 minutes or until it is just set. Allow to cool in the tin for a few minutes, then turn out, cut into wedges and serve hot, warm or at room temperature.

Sautéed garlic mushroom and parsley bruschetta

Serves 4
Preparation time: 15 minutes

4 thick slices sourdough bread
1 tablespoon olive oil
sea salt and freshly ground black pepper
30 g/1 oz butter
2 cloves garlic, finely chopped
250 g/8 oz mixed cultivated mushrooms, cleaned and sliced
2 tablespoons chopped flat-leaf parsley

This glamorous version of mushrooms on toast makes a tasty starter or light meal, or can be cut into smaller pieces and served with drinks.

Preheat a chargrill over a high heat. Brush both sides of each slice of bread with the olive oil and season well. Grill the bread for 2 minutes or until nicely scored by the grill. Turn over and repeat on the other side.

Melt the butter in a large frying pan placed over a high heat, then add the garlic and mushrooms and cook for 3–4 minutes. Take off the heat, add the parsley and season well. Place the mushrooms on the grilled bread and serve.

Wild mushroom and gruyère quiche

Serves 6–8
Preparation time: 45 minutes, plus 1 hour 30 minutes to prepare the pastry base

for the pastry:
120 g/4 oz plain flour
½ teaspoon fine sea salt
60 g/2 oz cold butter, cubed
1 large egg yolk
2 tablespoons cold water

for the filling:
30 g/1 oz butter
4 shallots, finely chopped
350 g/11½ oz mixed wild mushrooms, cleaned and
    cut or torn into small pieces
sea salt and freshly ground black pepper
250 ml/8 fl oz double cream
1 large eggs plus 1 yolk
90 g/3 oz gruyère cheese, grated

To make the pastry, place the flour, salt and butter in a food processor or mixer and whizz until it resembles fine breadcrumbs. Add the egg yolk and water and whizz briefly until the mixture comes together. Place on a lightly floured work surface and lightly knead with your hands, working it into a ball. Flatten lightly to form a large disc, cover with clingfilm and refrigerate for at least 45 minutes.

Preheat the oven to 180°C/350°F/gas mark 4. Take the pastry out of the fridge to bring it up to room temperature before attempting to roll it. Lightly flour a work surface and roll the pastry to fit a shallow 25 cm/10 in tart tin. Roll the pastry around a floured rolling pin and gently drape it over the tin. Carefully press it into place and prick the base with a fork. If any of the pastry tears it can be patched up with the offcuts. Place a large sheet of baking parchment over the pastry case and fill with baking beans. Place on a baking sheet and transfer to the oven. Cook for 15 minutes, then take out and remove the baking beans and parchment. Return to the oven for a further 10 minutes to crisp up the base. Remove from the oven and allow to cool slightly. Use a small knife to trim any excess pastry from around the rim and set aside while you prepare the filling.

To make the filling, place the butter in a large frying pan over a medium heat. Add the shallots and cook for 2 minutes or until they soften, then add the mushrooms and cook for a further 4 minutes or until they are soft and the moisture they release has evaporated. Take off the heat, season and set aside. Place the cream in a mixing bowl and whisk in the egg and yolk. Stir in the cheese and season. Scatter the mushrooms over the pastry base and cover with the creamy mixture. Place in the oven for 20 minutes, or until the filling has just set. Remove from the oven and allow the quiche to rest for a few minutes before cutting into wedges. Eat hot or warm with a mixed salad.

Beef, portabello mushroom and Guinness pie

Serves 6
Preparation time: 1 hour 30 minutes, plus 2½ hours to cook the beef

2 tablespoons plus 1 teaspoon groundnut oil
plain flour, seasoned
900 g/2 lb stewing beef, trimmed and cubed
250 ml/8 fl oz Guinness
1 carrot, peeled and cubed
1 large onion, peeled and sliced
175 g/6 oz portabello mushrooms, cut into large chunks
150 ml/5 fl oz beef or chicken stock
1 teaspoon Worcestershire sauce
4 thyme sprigs
1 bay leaf
sea salt and freshly ground black pepper
300 g/10 oz puff pastry
1 egg, lightly beaten

As with so many stewed dishes, the beef and mushroom mixture for this pie just gets better after a day or two. The filling can be made in advance and stored in the fridge. You can also make six individual pies, using small pie dishes.

Preheat the oven to 140°C/275°F/gas mark 1. Place a tablespoon of oil in a large frying pan set over a medium to high heat. Place the seasoned flour in a large bowl and add half the meat cubes. Toss well to coat each piece and shake to remove any excess flour. Place the meat in the pan, spacing the pieces well apart so they are not clumped together. If the meat is cooked in a large mass it is not able to brown properly. If your pan is not large enough you can cook the meat in a couple of batches. Cook for a few minutes until the base of the meat has a nice brown crust. Turn over and repeat on the other side. Transfer the meat to a large ovenproof casserole and repeat with the rest.

Pour a good splash of the Guinness into the frying pan and allow it to bubble. Scrape the base of the frying pan with a wooden spoon to remove any crusty bits at the bottom and pour it over the meat. Place the pan back on the heat and add a teaspoon of oil. Add the carrot and onion and cook for 2 minutes or until they start to soften and brown. Add the carrot and onion to the meat, then place the mushroom pieces in the pan for 2 minutes or until they colour. Add to the meat with the stock, Worcestershire sauce, thyme and bay leaf. Pour the remaining Guinness into the frying pan and bring up to a bubble. Stir well and scrape the base again, ensuring that all the sticky bits are loosened. Pour the liquid into the casserole and place it over a high heat until it comes up to a simmer. Season well, cover and place in the preheated oven for 2½ hours. Remove the casserole from the oven, taste and season the mixture if necessary. Set aside to cool while you prepare the pastry.

Set the oven to 220°C/425°F/gas mark 7. Lightly dust a work surface with flour. Roll out the pastry to fit the top of an ovenproof pie or baking dish large enough to accommodate the filling. Place the pie dish upside down on the pastry and cut round it with a sharp knife, allowing a small border of about 1½ cm/½ in. Trim off any excess pastry and discard. Transfer the rolled pastry to a lightly floured board or baking sheet and refrigerate for a minimum of 15 minutes.

Remove the thyme and bay leaf from the casserole and discard. Tip the mixture into the pie dish. Cover with the pastry and brush with the beaten egg. Use a fork to press down the edge of the pastry along the rim. Make a few slits through the top of the pastry to allow the air to escape. Place in the oven for 25 minutes, or until the pastry is puffy and golden and the filling is bubbling. Allow to cool slightly before serving.

Chargrilled sirloin steak and portabello mushroom baguette with pesto mayonnaise

Serves 4
Preparation time: 15 minutes

4 x 60 g/2 oz portabello mushrooms, cut into thick slices
1 teaspoon thyme leaves
2 tablespoons olive oil
sea salt and freshly ground black pepper
4 thin sirloin steaks, about 150 g/5 oz each
4 tablespoons mayonnaise
2 tablespoons pesto
1 baguette, cut into 4 lengths and halved lengthways
30 g/1 oz wild rocket (arugula) leaves

The steaks are best served rare to medium rare, but can be cooked a little longer if you prefer. You can also use mustard in place of the pesto and top the steaks with some grilled red onion wedges.

Preheat a chargrill over a very high heat. Place the mushroom slices in a bowl and toss with the thyme leaves and a tablespoon of olive oil. Place on the hot grill and cook for 1–2 minutes on each side or until they soften and colour. Transfer to a plate and season. Rub the remaining oil over the steaks, season, and place on the grill for 1–2 minutes, depending on whether you prefer them rare or medium rare. Turn them over and cook the other side for 1–2 minutes. Transfer to a plate and allow the steaks to rest for a few minutes, then trim off any excess fat.

Meanwhile, combine the mayonnaise and pesto and smear over the cut sides of the baguette lengths. Place the mushroom pieces over the base halves and top with a steak and a handful of rocket leaves. Replace the top halves and serve with lots of paper napkins.

Portabello mushroom burger with hummus and a parsley, mint and red onion salad

Serves 4
Preparation time: 30 minutes

4 large portabello mushrooms, about 90 g/ 3½ oz each
4 tablespoons olive oil
sea salt and freshly ground black pepper
4 ciabatta or focaccia rolls, halved

for the hummus:
175 g/6 oz chickpeas, drained
1 tablespoon tahini paste*
2 tablespoons lemon juice
1 clove garlic, mashed with a large pinch coarse sea salt
large pinch ground cumin
2 tablespoons water
sea salt and freshly ground black pepper

for the salad:
2 tablespoons roughly chopped flat-leaf parsley
2 tablespoons roughly chopped mint leaves
2 tablespoons finely diced red onion
30 g/1 oz wild rocket (arugula)
1 tablespoon lemon juice
1 tablespoon olive oil

* tahini paste is a sesame seed paste available from Middle Eastern grocers

Preheat the oven to 220°C/430°F/gas mark 7. Place the mushrooms gill side up on a lightly oiled roasting tin. Drizzle with the olive oil and season well. Place in the oven and cook for 10 minutes.

Meanwhile, whizz the hummus ingredients in a small food processor or mixer until combined. Taste and season well.

Place the salad ingredients in a bowl, season well and mix to combine. Smear the hummus over the rolls and top with a mushroom. Place the salad on top and eat straight away.

Crimini mushroom, prosciutto and artichoke pizza with taleggio cheese

Makes 4 x 30 cm/12 in pizzas
Preparation time: 1 hour, plus 1 hour proving time

for the dough:
750 g/1½ lb strong white flour, plus extra for dusting
1 sachet (7 g/½ oz) dried yeast
1 teaspoon fine sea salt
3 tablespoons extra virgin olive oil, plus extra for brushing

for the topping:
175 g/6 oz marinated artichokes in oil, thickly sliced
175 g/6 oz crimini mushrooms, thickly sliced
12 slices prosciutto
400 g/13 oz taleggio cheese, sliced
1½ tablespoons chopped rosemary leaves
freshly ground black pepper
4 tablespoons extra virgin olive oil

This is a light pizza based on the Italian pizza bianco, or 'white pizza', as it has an olive oil rather than a tomato base. The recipe makes four pizzas, but you can divide the dough and freeze any excess for later use. Simply thaw and roll as for fresh dough.

Place the flour, yeast and salt in a large mixing bowl. Add the oil and 400 ml/14 oz of tepid water. Mix the dough with your hands until everything is incorporated, then place on a lightly floured board. Knead for 8 minutes or until the dough is smooth and elastic. For a quicker dough you can place the dry mixture in a food processor or a mixer with a dough hook attached, then slowly pour in the liquid and process until the dough is stretchy and smooth. Brush a small amount of oil inside a large mixing bowl. Roll the dough into a ball on a lightly floured board, place in the bowl and cover loosely with a cloth. Transfer to a warm area for about an hour or until the dough has doubled in size. The rising time can vary depending on the room temperature.

Preheat the oven to its highest temperature. Knead the dough for a few minutes to beat out the air bubbles that formed with the rising. Cut the dough into four even-sized pieces. Using your hands, shape one of the pieces of dough into a rough disc and place on a lightly floured work surface. Roll the dough into a thin 30 cm/12 in circle using a lightly floured rolling pin. Transfer to a lightly oiled baking sheet and repeat with the other three pieces of dough if you have enough baking sheets. If you don't, you can roll out the pieces of dough, flour them well, and stack them between layers of clingfilm or greaseproof paper until needed.

Scatter the artichokes and mushrooms over the bases. Lay the prosciutto slices over the top and cover with the cheese. Sprinkle the rosemary leaves on top, season well with pepper, and drizzle the oil over. Place one or two pizzas on the highest shelf of the oven and cook for 10 minutes or until the bases are crispy and golden. Repeat with the remaining pizzas and eat straight from the oven as soon as each batch is ready.

When it comes to cleaning your mushrooms, it's important to remember that they should not be soaked as they are porous and will become waterlogged. If you must wash mushrooms only do so with firm tight capped cultivated mushrooms, such as button mushrooms. Wash them briefly under water and pat dry to remove any excess moisture. Wash your mushrooms just before use as the process will shorten their storage life. Generally, mushrooms only need cleaning if there is visible dirt, which is often the case with wild mushrooms. Simply wipe them gently with a lightly moistened cloth or brush clean with a pastry brush. Any stubborn compacted dirt can be removed with a knife tip. Contrary to popular belief there is no need to peel mushrooms. This is a waste of time (and mushroom!).

Porcini mushroom, rosemary and olive oil focaccia

Makes 1 large sheet about 30 x 40 cm (12 x 16 in)
Preparation time: 1 hour plus 1 hour proving time

750 g/1½ lb strong white flour, plus extra for dusting
1 sachet (7 g/½ oz) dried yeast
4 teaspoons sea salt flakes
130 ml/4½ fl oz fruity extra virgin olive oil
280 g/9 oz porcini mushrooms, sliced
4 tablespoons rosemary leaves
sea salt and freshly ground black pepper

This fragrant bread has many uses. For a dinner accompaniment, try cutting it into long fingers and serving alongside a small bowl of olive oil for dipping. For a tasty sandwich cut it into large squares, split it lengthways and fill it with slices of prosciutto and mozzarella. It can also be roughly torn and served as part of an antipasti.

Place the flour, yeast and half the salt into a large mixing bowl. Mix 3 tablespoons of the oil with 400 ml/14 fl oz of tepid water and add to the dry mixture. Mix the dough with your hands until everything is incorporated, then transfer to a very lightly floured board and knead for 8 minutes or until it is smooth and stretchy. For a quicker result you can place the dry mixture into a mixer or food processor with the dough hook attached, then slowly pour in the liquid and process until the dough is smooth and elastic. Brush a small amount of the remaining oil inside a large mixing bowl. Roll the dough into a ball and place in the oiled bowl, covering with a cloth. Transfer to a warm place and allow it to rise until it has doubled in size. This should take about an hour, but can vary depending on the room temperature.

Meanwhile, place a tablespoon of the remaining oil into a large frying pan over a medium heat. Add half the sliced porcini mushrooms in a single layer and cook for 1 minute on each side or until they soften but don't colour. Season well and transfer to a plate. Add another tablespoon of oil to the pan. Cook the rest of the mushrooms, add them to the first batch, season and allow to cool.

Preheat the oven to the highest temperature. Chop half the rosemary leaves and leave the rest whole. Place a large flat 30 x 40 cm/12 x 16 in baking sheet in the oven to heat. Place the risen dough on a lightly floured board. Roughly roll to create a large surface area and scatter over the chopped rosemary. Knead the dough well to incorporate the rosemary and to 'knock out' the air bubbles that made the dough rise. Roll or stretch out into a rough thin rectangle about the size of the baking sheet. Using your fingertips, make random indents in the dough. Remove the hot baking sheet from the oven and drizzle over a tablespoon of the remaining oil, shaking it well to cover the base. Transfer the dough to the hot baking sheet. Working quickly, lay the mushroom slices over the dough and scatter the whole rosemary leaves over the top. Sprinkle with 2 teaspoons of sea salt flakes and drizzle over the remaining oil. Place in the oven and cook for 15 minutes or until the base sounds hollow when tapped. Allow the focaccia to cool slightly on the baking sheet then cut it into wedges.

Meat
and Fish

Guinea fowl and trompettes de mort mushroom casserole

Serves 4-6
Preparation time: 40 minutes, plus 1 hour in the oven

16 shallots
1 tablespoon olive oil
90 g/3½ oz smoked pancetta, cubed
seasoned flour for dusting
2 x 1 kg/2 lb guinea fowl, each jointed into 8 pieces
2 cloves garlic, chopped
3 tablespoons brandy
300 ml/½ pint red wine
150 ml/5 fl oz well-seasoned chicken stock
4 sprigs thyme
2 bay leaves
30 g/1 oz butter
200 g/7 oz trompettes de mort, cleaned and torn
    into even-sized pieces
sea salt and freshly ground black pepper

Although light in consistency, this casserole has a wonderful depth of flavour. The sauce is thin rather than thick and floury. As it has a lot of sauce it is especially suited to absorbent accompaniments such as mashed potatoes or rice. Chanterelle mushrooms also work well if trompettes de mort are not available.

Place the shallots in a bowl, cover with boiling water for a minute to loosen the skins, then peel, using a small knife.

Place the oil in a large casserole over a medium to high heat. Add the shallots and cook for 4 minutes or until nicely browned. Remove with a slotted spoon and transfer to a large bowl. Add the pancetta to the casserole and cook for 4 minutes or until browned and crispy. Transfer to the bowl with the shallots, using a slotted spoon. Take the casserole off the heat, leaving the fat inside.

Preheat the oven to 150°C/300°F/gas mark 2. Place the flour in a large bowl and add the guinea fowl pieces. Mix well to cover each piece, then shake off any excess flour. Place the casserole back over a high heat and fry half of the guinea fowl pieces for 3 minutes on each side or until browned. Transfer to the bowl with the shallots and pancetta and repeat with the second batch, adding the garlic at the last minute. Pour the brandy into the casserole and light with a match, standing well back to allow the flames to subside. Add the wine, bring up to the boil, and add the reserved browned ingredients from the bowl, plus the stock, thyme and bay leaves. Bring to a simmer, then cover and place in the oven for an hour.

Meanwhile, place the butter in a frying pan set over a high heat, add the mushrooms, and cook for a few minutes or until they soften. Season well, then set aside until needed.

Take the casserole out of the oven and remove the guinea fowl pieces with tongs. Place them in a warmed serving bowl, cover with foil and set the casserole over a high heat for a few minutes to reduce the sauce slightly. It should not be too thick, but if you prefer it a little thicker, just reduce it for a longer time. Add the cooked mushrooms, stir well and season. Pour over the guinea fowl pieces and serve.

Thyme scented roasted pheasant with crimini mushrooms, crème fraîche and cider sauce

Serves 4
Preparation time: 1 hour

30 g/1 oz butter
1 tablespoon chopped thyme leaves
2 pheasants, about 1 kg/2lb each
250 g/8 oz crimini mushrooms, cleaned and quartered
150 ml/5 fl oz dry cider
120 g/4 oz crème fraîche
sea salt and freshly ground black pepper

Preheat the oven to 190°C /375°F/gas mark 5. Roughly mash the butter and thyme together with a fork and smear over the pheasants. Season well, transfer them to a large roasting tin and place in the oven for 30 minutes, basting the birds halfway through the cooking time. Remove from the oven and add the mushroom pieces. Stir well to coat with the roasting juices and put back into the oven for another 12 minutes or until the birds are cooked through.

Transfer the pheasants on to a plate, leaving the mushrooms and roasting juices in the tin. Loosely cover the birds with foil to keep them warm, and set aside to allow them to rest for 10 minutes.

Meanwhile, place the roasting tin over a high heat on the stove and add the cider. Allow it to bubble away, then scrape the base with a wooden spoon to remove the residue. Cook for 3 minutes, then turn the heat down to low. Add the crème fraîche, stir to combine, season well, then take off the heat. Joint or carve each bird and place on a warmed platter. Pour the sauce over the meat or serve separately. Serve with some steamed greens and roast potatoes.

Venison sausages braised with porcini mushrooms, red wine and sage

Serves 4
Preparation time: 45 minutes

45 g/2 oz dried porcini mushrooms
1 tablespoon olive oil
750 g/1½ lb venison sausages
1 large red onion, peeled and sliced
12 sage leaves
1 bay leaf
275 ml/9 fl oz red wine
100 ml/3½ fl oz beef or chicken stock
15 g/½ oz cold butter, cubed
sea salt and freshly ground black pepper
2 tablespoons chopped flat-leaf parsley

The earthy gaminess of this braised dish makes it perfect, hearty dish for when the weather turns cold.

Place the dried mushrooms in a bowl and cover with warm water. Leave for 20 minutes, then remove from the water and squeeze dry. Set the mushrooms aside and discard the water.

Place the oil into a large sauté pan over a medium to high heat. Add the sausages and cook for 3–4 minutes on each side or until they are well browned all over. Transfer to a plate and set aside. Add the onion, sage and bay leaf to the pan and cook for 3–4 minutes or until the onions soften and begin to colour. Return the sausages to the pan and add the wine and stock, scraping the base of the pan with a wooden spoon to remove the sticky bits that are full of flavour. Bring up to the boil, cook for a minute and add the mushrooms. Cover the pan and turn down the heat to maintain a very gentle simmer. Cook for 30 minutes, then remove the lid. Transfer the sausages to a plate and keep warm. Stir the butter into the sauce, turn up the heat and cook for 5 minutes to allow the liquid to bubble and reduce slightly. Put the sausages back in the pan, season well, sprinkle the parsley on top and serve with wet polenta or creamy mashed potatoes.

Chicken supreme stuffed with dried porcini mushrooms, rosemary and goat's cheese

Serves 4
Preparation time: 1 hour

15 g/½ oz dried porcini mushrooms
1½ teaspoons rosemary leaves, finely chopped
150 g/5 oz soft, rindless mild goat's cheese
zest of 1 lemon
4 x 175 g/6 oz free-range or organic chicken supremes,
   skin on
15 g/½ oz butter
salt and freshly ground black pepper
2 teaspoons olive oil

Soak the mushrooms in a bowl of warm water for 20 minutes.

Preheat the oven to 220°C/425°F/gas mark 7. Remove the soaked mushrooms and squeeze dry. Discard the liquid or strain it for use in a risotto. Roughly chop the mushrooms and place in a bowl with the rosemary, goat's cheese and lemon zest. Season to taste and mix to a smooth paste.

Place a chicken breast on a board with the skin side facing up. Using a long thin knife, make a horizontal pocket in the breast, parallel to the board, starting along one of the longer sides. Make the slit through the breast as deep as possible but do not cut all the way through. Repeat with the rest of the breasts. Push a quarter of the goat's cheese mixture into each incision. Allow a small border with no filling at the opening to prevent it spilling out when cooked. Secure each with a couple of cocktail sticks, then season on both sides.

Heat a large (preferably ovenproof) frying pan over a medium heat and add the butter and olive oil. Place the breasts in the pan, skin-side down, and cook for 5 minutes or until the skin colours. Gently turn over and cook for another 2 minutes. Transfer the pan to the oven (if it's ovenproof) and cook for 8 minutes. If your pan is not ovenproof you can transfer the chicken to a roasting tin, allowing a few more minutes' cooking time. Take out of the oven and rest for 2–3 minutes. Serve with sautéed potatoes and a green salad.

Veal escalopes with pied de mouton mushrooms, sorrel and cognac

Serves 2
Preparation time: 20 minutes

3 tablespoons plain flour
sea salt and freshly ground black pepper
2 x 150 g/5 oz veal escalopes, beaten until thin
1 tablespoon olive oil
15 g/½ oz butter
120 g/4 oz pied de mouton mushrooms, cleaned and sliced
3 tablespoons cognac
15 g/½ oz sorrel leaves, shredded
4 tablespoons double cream

You could use pied bleu mushrooms instead of pied de mouton, as they are equally dense and meaty.

Place the flour on a large plate. Season the escalopes, then lay one of them in the flour, dredging well to cover and shaking to remove any excess. Transfer to another plate and repeat with the remaining escalope.

Place the oil and butter in a large frying pan over a medium heat. Add the floured escalopes and cook for 2 minutes on each side or until lightly browned and just cooked through. Remove from the pan and set aside. Add the mushrooms to the pan and cook for 2 minutes or until browned and softened, then add the cognac and cook for half a minute or until most of the liquid has disappeared. Add the sorrel, stir until wilted, then add the cream and stir in. Put the meat back in the pan to warm it through. Taste and season, then transfer to two warm plates and serve with rice or sautéed potatoes and some wilted greens.

Beef Wellington

Serves 4 generously
Preparation time: 1 hour 30 minutes

30 g/1 oz butter
4 shallots, finely chopped
1 clove garlic, finely chopped
300 g/10 oz mix of wild and cultivated mushrooms,
    cleaned and very finely diced
2 tablespoons cognac
1 tablespoon groundnut oil
800 g/1¾ lb piece fillet steak, trimmed (taken from the
    thick end of the fillet)
300 g/10 oz puff pastry, preferably made with butter
1 tablespoon Dijon mustard
1 egg, beaten
sea salt and freshly ground black pepper

The combination of fragrant mushrooms and tender
beef fillet is a delight. When combined with a flaky
buttery pastry, drenched with the heavenly juices, it
becomes truly irresistible.

Place the butter in a large pan over a low to medium heat.
Once melted, add the shallots, cook for 3 minutes, then add
the garlic and cook for a further 2 minutes or until softened
but not coloured. Add the mushrooms and cook for 10
minutes or until they soften and become dry, stirring every
now and then. Turn up the heat, add the cognac and cook
for a minute to allow the liquid to evaporate. Season well and
set aside to cool while you prepare the meat.

Put the oil into a frying pan over a high heat. Place the
meat in the pan, searing for a minute on each side or until a
rich brown crust forms. Sear the ends of the meat, then
transfer to a plate and set aside to cool.

Preheat the oven to 220°C/425°F/gas mark 7. Roll the
pastry on a lightly floured board into a rectangle measuring
about 30 x 35 cm/12 x 14 in. These dimensions are only a
guide: the dimensions of the meat will vary according to its
thickness, which will in turn dictate the size of the pastry
piece required. Make sure the rectangle will generously
envelop the meat and mushrooms and allow for the sides
of the pastry to be tucked underneath.

Position the pastry with its shorter edge facing you and
smear with the mustard, leaving a 5 cm/2 in border. Brush
the border with the beaten egg. Place two-thirds of the
mushrooms over the mustard. Liberally season the seared
meat and place legthways along the middle of the pastry.
Lay the remaining mushrooms over the meat and press
lightly with your palms to keep the mixture in place. Bring
the long, bottom pastry edge upwards towards the middle
of the meat. Take the long edge from the top of the pastry
and fold it downwards, completely covering the meat. There
will now be a horizontal seam running across the pastry.
Firmly press down on the two shorter sides to seal them
together, and brush the top with some beaten egg. Fold the
two short sides upward and press down to seal them to the
seamed side. Gently turn over and position, seams down,
on a lightly oiled baking sheet. Brush with some more beaten
egg and place in the oven for 35 minutes, by which time the
pastry will be lovely and golden and the meat will be medium
rare. Take out of the oven and leave to rest for 10 minutes,
then transfer to a carving board. Cut into thick slices and
serve with sautéed new potatoes and some buttered greens.

Lebanese spiced lamb, almonds and portabello mushrooms

Serves 4-6
Preparation time: 45 minutes, plus marinating time

350 g/12 oz lamb leg meat, trimmed and cubed
2 tablespoons olive oil
2 teaspoons mixed spice
45 g/1¾ oz butter
1 large onion, finely sliced
250 g/8 oz paella rice
large pinch saffron
1 cinnamon stick
3 wide strips of lemon zest
500 ml/17 fl oz chicken stock
sea salt and freshly ground black pepper
90 g/3 oz flaked almonds
200 g/7 oz portabello mushrooms, sliced
large handful coriander (cilantro), roughly chopped

Put the meat in a bowl, add half the olive oil, the mixed spice and stir to combine. Set aside to marinate for 30 minutes.

Gently heat 15 g/½ oz butter in a pan. Add the onion and cook for 2–3 minutes or until softened. Increase the heat and stir in the rice, saffron, cinnamon and lemon zest. Add the stock and ¾ teaspoon of salt and bring to the boil. Stir, cover and lower the heat to a simmer. Cook for 10 minutes, turn off the heat and leave for another 10 minutes.

Meanwhile, place another 15 g/½ oz of butter in a large frying pan over a medium heat. Add the almonds and cook for a few minutes, stirring, until they brown. Tip into a bowl and put the pan over a high heat. Add the remaining butter and the mushrooms and cook for 4 minutes or until they brown. Remove them from the pan and set aside. Add the remaining olive oil to the pan, then the lamb. Fry for 4 minutes or until the meat browns, then add to the mushrooms.

Put the mushrooms and lamb in the pan with the cooked rice and stir to combine. Season well and add half the almonds and coriander. Stir again and transfer to a warm plate. Scatter over the remaining almonds and coriander, and serve.

Steamed sea bass with oyster and enoki mushrooms

Serves 2
Preparation time: 20 minutes

1 teaspoon sesame oil
60 g/2 oz oyster mushrooms, sliced or torn into pieces
60 g/2 oz enoki mushrooms, separated
2 x 150 g/5 oz sea bass fillets, skin on and bones removed
salt and ground white pepper
1 tablespoon very finely shredded ginger
2 spring onions (scallions), finely sliced diagonally
1 teaspoon soy sauce
1 teaspoon sake*
1 tablespoon lime juice
small handful coriander (cilantro) leaves

*available from Oriental grocers

This quick and healthy dish is full of the refreshing flavours of spring onion, ginger, lime and coriander. Season with a little soy sauce to taste and serve with steamed rice and stir-fried Chinese greens.

You can use use two small whole cleaned sea bass instead of fillets. Make three deep diagonal slashes on either side of the fish and cook for a few more minutes.

Place a large steaming basket and lid over a pan of water on a medium heat. Brush a heatproof plate (large enough to hold the fish and fit in the steamer) with ½ teaspoon of sesame oil and cover with the mushrooms. Season the fish well with salt and white pepper and place on top of the mushrooms. Scatter the ginger and half the spring onions over the fish, and place the plate in the steamer. Mix the soy sauce, sake and lime juice together in a small bowl and pour the mixture over the fish. Replace the lid and steam for 8 minutes or until the fish is cooked through, then carefully remove the whole plate from the steamer. Drizzle with the remaining sesame oil, scatter the coriander leaves and remaining spring onions on top and serve.

Crispy sea bream with black bean and hon-shimeji stir-fry

Serves 2
Preparation time: 25 minutes

1 tablespoon salted dried black beans*
2 tablespoons chicken stock
1 tablespoon oyster sauce
1 tablespoon Chinese rice wine*
½ teaspoon sugar
2 x 150 g/5 oz sea bream fillets, skin on and bones removed
1 tablespoon groundnut oil, plus extra for brushing
75 g/3 oz baby corn, halved lengthways
½ stick celery, sliced diagonally
75 g/3 oz hon-shimeji mushrooms, separated and halved if large
1 teaspoon minced ginger
1 clove garlic, chopped
1 large spring onion, sliced diagonally
1 teaspoon sesame oil
salt and ground white pepper

*available from Oriental grocers

Soak the black beans in water for 5 minutes to remove some of the saltiness, then squeeze dry, place in a small bowl and mash with a fork. Add the chicken stock, oyster sauce, rice wine and sugar, stir to combine, then set aside.

Place a large non-stick frying pan over a high heat. Brush the fillets with oil and season with salt and white pepper. Place in the pan, skin side down, and cook for 3 minutes or until the skin is crispy and brown. Turn over and cook for a further 2 minutes, then transfer to a plate and keep warm.

Place a wok over a high heat and add the oil. Add the baby corn, celery and mushrooms and cook for a minute, then add the ginger and garlic and cook for 30 seconds more. Pour in the black bean sauce, add the spring onions and cook for another 30 seconds, stirring well throughout. Take off the heat and add the sesame oil. Divide between two warm plates and place the fish on top with the crispy side facing up.

Steamed squid stuffed with minced pork and dried cloud ears

Serves 2
Preparation time: 50 minutes

2 dried cloud ears (also known as black fungus)*
120 g/4 oz minced pork
1 clove garlic, chopped
1 spring onion, finely sliced
1 teaspoon finely chopped coriander stalks, taken from the root end
¼ teaspoon sugar
½ teaspoon fish sauce*
¼ teaspoon sesame oil
large pinch ground white pepper
6 small to medium squid tubes (about 250 g/8 oz in total), cleaned
groundnut oil for brushing the squid
sweet chilli sauce*, to serve
a handful coriander (cilantro) leaves, to serve

* available from Oriental grocers

Place the dried cloud ears in a bowl, cover with boiling water for 10 minutes, and leave to soften. Remove them from the water, trim off any hard bits and finely slice.

Put the pork, garlic, spring onion, coriander root, sugar, fish sauce and sesame oil in a bowl. Add the sliced cloud ears, season with the ground white pepper and mix well.

Place a large steaming basket with a lid over a pan of simmering water. Using a teaspoon, stuff the squid tubes with the pork mixture and secure the opening with a toothpick. Each tube should be about three-quarters full. Lightly brush with oil and place in the steamer. Cover and cook for 20 minutes.

Take the stuffed squid out of the steamer and carefully remove each toothpick. Allow to cool slightly, then slice into pieces to reveal the cross-section. Place the slices on a serving plate, drizzle with the sweet chilli sauce, scatter the coriander leaves over the top and serve.

Roasted wild salmon fillets with girolle mushrooms and gremolata

Serves 2
Preparation time: 20 minutes

2 x 150 g/5 oz wild salmon fillets, skin on and bones
    removed
1 tablespoon olive oil, plus extra for brushing
sea salt and freshly ground black pepper
15 g/½ oz butter
150 g/5 oz girolle mushrooms, cleaned and thickly sliced
1 tablespoon grated lemon zest
1 small clove garlic, finely chopped
2 tablespoons chopped flat-leaf parsley
juice of ½ lemon
lemon wedges to serve

Preheat the oven to 220°C/430°F/gas mark 7. Brush the fish
fillets with olive oil, season well and place on a baking tray.
Place on the top shelf of the oven and cook for 8 minutes or
until the flesh is just slightly undercooked. It will cook a
little further with the heat it retains.

Meanwhile, place the olive oil and butter in a large
saucepan over a high heat and add the mushrooms. Cook
for 3 minutes or until they soften, then add the lemon zest
and garlic and cook for 30 seconds. Take off the heat, add
the parsley and lemon juice to taste, then season.

Place the salmon fillets on a warm serving plate. Pour the
mushrooms over the top and serve with lemon wedges and
a lightly dressed rocket (arugula) salad.

Prawn, hon-shimeji and shiitake mushroom stir fry with pak choi and oyster sauce

Serves 2
Preparation time: 15 minutes

for the sauce:
2 tablespoons oyster sauce
1 tablespoon sake*
1 teaspoon soy sauce
1 tablespoon water
½ teaspoon sugar

for the stir fry:
2 tablespoons groundnut oil
12 large raw prawns (shrimp), shelled and deveined
1 small clove garlic, finely chopped
½ teaspoon finely chopped ginger
45 g/2 oz hon-shimeji mushrooms, separated
45 g/2 oz shiitake mushrooms, tough stalks removed,
    quartered
90 g/3 oz pak choi (or other Chinese greens), washed
    and sliced
1 spring onion, finely sliced
steamed rice, to serve

*available from Japanese grocers

Make the sauce by mixing the ingredients together in a
small bowl. Set aside until needed.

Place half the oil into a large wok over a high heat.
Add the prawns and cook for 2 minutes or until cooked
through. Transfer to a plate and add the remaining oil to
the pan. Add the garlic, ginger and mushrooms and cook
for 1–2 minutes or until they colour and soften. Place the
prawns and pak choi in the pan, toss and add the sauce.
Cook for a further minute and top with the spring onions.
Transfer to a warm serving bowl and serve with steamed rice.

Oyster mushroom, smoked trout and leek filled crêpes

Serves 4
Preparation time: 1 hour 30 minutes

For the crêpe batter:
2 large eggs
75 g/3 oz plain flour
180 ml/6 fl oz milk
2 tablespoons melted butter
¼ teaspoon fine sea salt
2 teaspoons seeded mustard
olive oil for brushing the crêpe pan

For the sauce:
30 g/1 oz butter, plus a little extra for greasing the
    baking dish
1 level tablespoon plain flour
250 ml/8 fl oz milk, warmed
1 tablespoon seeded mustard
60 g/2 oz Cheddar cheese, grated, plus 15 g/½ oz for
    sprinkling on top
sea salt and freshly ground black pepper

For the filling:
30 g/1 oz butter
1 large leek, washed, trimmed and finely sliced
200 g/7 oz oyster mushrooms, torn into even-sized pieces
4 tablespoons white wine
150 g/5 oz smoked trout fillets, skin and bones removed,
    flaked into large chunks
2 tablespoons crème fraîche
sea salt and freshly ground black pepper

To make the crêpes, place the ingredients in a blender and
whizz until smooth. Pour into a jug, cover and leave to rest
for at least 30 minutes while you prepare the sauce and filling.

To cook the crêpes, place an 18 cm/7 in non-stick crêpe
pan or frying pan over a medium heat and brush or spray

lightly with the oil. Pour 2–2½ tablespoons of the batter into
the pan and swirl the pan around to distribute the batter
thinly. Cook for a minute or so, until lightly browned
underneath, then gently turn over using a spatula. Cook for
a further minute or until cooked, and set aside on a plate.
Repeat until you have eight crêpes, stacking them as they are
cooked. There will be a small amount of mixture left over,
which you can use if you need it.

To make the sauce, melt the butter in a small pan over a
medium heat. Add the flour and stir or whisk to combine
until smooth. Cook for 2 minutes, stirring a few times.
Add a splash of the warm milk and whisk or stir until
smooth. Gradually add the rest of the milk in small amounts,
stirring until smooth between each addition. If you add too
much milk at once the sauce can become lumpy. Cook for a
few minutes, stirring often, until the sauce thickens. Add the
mustard and cheese and stir until the cheese melts. Cook for
a few more minutes to further thicken the sauce. Season well
and set aside until needed.

To make the filling, place half the butter in a large frying
pan set over a medium heat. Add the leeks and cook for
3 minutes or until softened, then transfer to a mixing bowl.
Place the remaining butter in the pan and add the
mushrooms, cooking for a further 3 minutes or until
softened and lightly browned. Add the wine and cook until
it evaporates. Transfer to the bowl with the leeks and add the
flaked fish. Add the crème fraîche, season, and gently mix
together, being careful not to break up the chunks of fish.

To assemble and cook the crêpes, preheat the oven to
200°C/400°F/gas mark 6 and lightly brush a gratin or
baking dish with butter. Place a crêpe on a board and spoon
an eighth of the filling mixture into the middle. Fold the
bottom flap up and the top flap down and turn the ends in
to create an enclosed parcel. Place on a plate and repeat with
the remaining crêpes. Arrange the crêpes over the base of the
buttered dish seam sides down, pour the sauce over the top
(it may be quite thick if it has cooled) and scatter with the
grated cheese. Place in the oven and cook for 20 minutes or
until the top is browned and bubbling. Remove from the
oven and allow to stand for a few minutes before serving.
Eat hot or warm with a green salad and some crusty bread.

Egg nets with fragrant seafood and shiitake mushroom stir-fry

Serves 4
Preparation time: 45 minutes

for the sauce:
1 red chilli, deseeded and finely chopped
1 clove garlic, finely chopped
2 tablespoons lime juice
2 tablespoons sugar
3 tablespoons Thai fish sauce*
3 tablespoons rice wine vinegar*
2 tablespoons water
2 teaspoons finely chopped coriander stalks, taken from the root end
large pinch ground white pepper

for the egg nets:
2 large eggs
1 teaspoon groundnut oil

for the filling:
4 tablespoons groundnut oil
180 g/6 oz shiitake mushrooms, tough stalks removed, sliced
120 g/4 oz raw peeled prawns (shrimp), roughly chopped
120 g/4 oz queen scallops, wiped dry
120 g/4 oz baby squid tubes, wiped dry and finely sliced
4 lime leaves, very finely sliced*
60 g/2 oz beansprouts
45 g/1½ oz cashew nuts or peanuts, roasted and chopped
1 red chilli, deseeded and finely sliced
4 Thai purple shallots, peeled and finely sliced*
handful whole coriander (cilantro) leaves
handful whole mint leaves
lime wedges, to serve

* available from Oriental grocers

These fine egg nets are complemented by a punchy sauce that promises a simultaneous hit of sour, sweet, salty and spicy flavours. The egg nets don't have to be lacy. Instead, just pour some of the beaten egg into the pan and swirl it around to make a thin crêpe.

Make the sauce by combining the ingredients in a bowl and stirring to dissolve the sugar. Set aside until needed.

To make the egg nets, whisk the eggs well and strain through a wide-meshed sieve . Place a wok or large non-stick frying pan over a high heat and lightly brush with some oil. Place the strained eggs into a squeezy plastic bottle with a fine spout (a leftover ketchup container is ideal). If the spout is not very fine you can just place your finger over part of it. Pour a quarter of the egg into the hot pan by wiggling the bottle from a height to create a lacy effect. The mixture shouldn't completely cover the base of the pan. Cook for a minute or until the egg sets. Carefully remove the egg net and place it on a piece of baking parchment. Cover with another piece of parchment. Brush the frying pan with oil and cook three more egg nets. Cover and set aside.

To make the filling, place a large pan or wok over a high heat. Add half of the oil and the mushrooms and cook for 2–3 minutes or until they brown. Transfer to a bowl and add the remaining oil to the pan. Tip in the seafood and cook for 2 minutes. Return the mushrooms and 90 ml/3 fl oz of the sauce and cook for a further minute. Take off the heat and add the lime leaves, beansprouts, nuts, chilli and shallots. Add half the coriander and mint leaves and stir through.

To serve, place an egg net on a plate and place a quarter of the filling over one half. Fold the other half over and repeat with the other egg nets. Serve garnished with the remaining herbs and some lime wedges. Pass the remaining sauce round at the table.

Eggs and Vegetables

Parmesan crusted wild mushroom soufflé

Serves 4
Preparation time: 1 hour

45 g/1½ oz butter, plus some melted butter for greasing the
    ramekins
45 g/1½ oz Parmesan cheese, very finely grated
1 shallot, peeled and finely chopped
1 small clove garlic, finely chopped
150 g/5 oz mixed wild mushrooms, cleaned and cut or torn
    into small pieces
sea salt and freshly ground black pepper
2 tablespoons plain flour
200 ml/7 fl oz milk, warmed
a few fresh grindings of nutmeg
5 large egg whites and 1 yolk

For a luxurious finishing touch, try topping each
serving of soufflé with a dollop of thick cream,
mascarpone or crème fraîche.

You can also divide the soufflé mixture between
six smaller ramekins if you take a few minutes off
the cooking time.

Lightly brush 4 x 250 ml/8 oz soufflé dishes with the melted
butter. Place 2 tablespoons of Parmesan into one of the
buttered dishes and shake well to dust the cheese evenly over
the butter. Tip the excess cheese into the next dish and repeat
until all four are lightly and evenly coated. Transfer to a
baking sheet and refrigerate until needed.

Place 15g/½ oz of the butter into a large pan placed over
a medium heat. Add the shallots and garlic and cook for
2 minutes or until softened. Turn up the heat and add the
mushrooms. Cook for 4 minutes, stirring often until they
soften and the liquid evaporates. Take the pan off the heat,
season the mushrooms well and set aside to cool.

Preheat the oven to 190°C/375°F/gas mark 5. Place the
remaining butter in a small pan and melt over a medium
heat. Add the flour and stir or whisk to combine until
smooth. Cook for 1 minute, stirring often. Add a splash
of the warm milk and stir or whisk until smooth. Gradually
add the rest of the milk in small amounts, beating until
smooth between batches. If you add too much milk at once
the sauce can become lumpy. Cook, stirring often, until it
thickens. Add the cheese and stir the sauce until it is smooth
and very thick. Cook for another minute, season with the
nutmeg, salt and pepper, and set aside to cool.

Finely chop the softened mushrooms and place in a large
mixing bowl. Add the egg yolk to the cheese sauce and stir
until combined, then add the sauce to the chopped
mushrooms and mix well.

Place the egg whites and a pinch of salt in a large mixing
bowl. Using an electric beater, whisk the whites until stiff.
Place about a third of the whites in the bowl with the
mushroom sauce and fold it in to loosen the mixture. Add
the remaining whites and gently fold in until the mixture
is incorporated. Be careful not to overdo it, as the air will
escape if the mixture is over-handled. Divide the mixture
between the prepared soufflé dishes and transfer to the oven
for 18 minutes, by which time the soufflés will be browned
and well risen. Don't be tempted to open the oven for a peek
as they can collapse quickly. Serve immediately.

Portabello mushroom, Parmesan and mascarpone omelette

Serves 1 generously
Preparation time: 15 minutes

20 g/⅔ oz butter
60 g/2 oz portabello mushrooms, sliced
sea salt and freshly ground black pepper
3 medium or large eggs, lightly beaten
1 tablespoon mascarpone
1 tablespoon grated Parmesan cheese
1 heaped teaspoon roughly chopped flat-leaf parsley

You can use just one of the cheeses or omit the cheese altogether if you prefer a lighter omelette.

Place about three-quarters of the butter (there's no need to be exact) into a small omelette pan placed over a medium heat. Add the mushrooms once the butter begins to foam and cook for 3 minutes or until softened and browned. Remove from the heat, season and place in a small bowl. Turn the heat up to medium high, wipe the pan out and place back over the heat. Add the remaining butter and allow it to foam. Season the eggs and add them to the pan. As soon as the sides begin to cook, use a wooden spoon or spatula to scrape the base of the pan from the perimeter inwards, tilting the pan as you do so to allow the egg to run into the spaces that this creates. Do this for 1–2 minutes, or until the base is set and the top is just very slightly undercooked (it will carry on cooking in its own heat). Take off the heat and place the mushrooms in a row along the middle of the eggs. Top with the mascarpone, Parmesan and parsley and fold the sides inwards to fully enclose the filling. Slide on to a warm plate and eat immediately.

Mixed mushroom, courgette and Parmesan frittata

Serves 4
Preparation time: 30 minutes

2 tablespoons olive oil
225 g/8 oz mixed mushrooms, cleaned and thickly sliced
1 medium courgette (zucchini), trimmed and sliced diagonally into eight
6 large eggs
sea salt and freshly ground black pepper
60 g/2 oz Parmesan cheese, grated
30 g/1 oz butter

Place a tablespoon of olive oil into a 25 cm/10 in non-stick ovenproof frying pan and set over a medium to high heat. Add the mushrooms and cook for 4 minutes or until they soften and brown. Transfer to a large plate and set aside. Add the remaining oil to the pan and add the courgettes, cooking for 2 minutes on each side or until lightly browned. Place on the plate with the mushrooms, season well and allow to cool slightly.

Preheat a grill to medium. Break the eggs into a large mixing bowl and beat with the cheese. Add the mushrooms and courgettes, season and mix well. Place the pan over a low heat and add the butter. Once melted, swirl it around the pan and tip in the egg mixture. Cook for 10 minutes, or until the sides set and the middle is still wobbly. Place under the grill for 3 minutes or until the middle of the frittata has just set. Turn out on to a serving plate and serve hot, warm or at room temperature.

Muffins topped with mushrooms, poached eggs and hollandaise sauce

Serves 2–4
Preparation time: 40 minutes

for the hollandaise sauce:
2 large egg yolks
1 tablespoon white wine vinegar
125 g/4 oz cold butter, cubed
salt and cayenne pepper

15 g/½ oz butter
1 tablespoon olive oil
250 g/8 oz cultivated mushrooms (try field, portabello,
    crimini or button), sliced
½ teaspoon thyme leaves, chopped
sea salt and freshly ground black pepper
1 tablespoon white wine vinegar
4 large eggs
2 muffins, each sliced in half, or 4 thick slices of
    sourdough bread
2 tablespoons chives, cut into small lengths

For a salty kick, this Sunday morning brunch dish can be topped with a few crispy strips of smoked bacon.

To make the hollandaise sauce, place the egg yolks and vinegar in a double boiler or heatproof bowl set over a pan of barely simmering water. Do not allow the base of the bowl to come into contact with the hot water. Whisk or stir until the mixture begins to thicken, then add a cube of the cold butter and whisk or stir until it is combined. Continue to add the butter cubes, a few at a time, until they are incorporated and the sauce is thick and glossy. Season with salt and cayenne pepper and take off the heat, leaving the bowl on top of the pan of water. The sauce will stay warm while you prepare the mushrooms.

Place the butter and olive oil in a large frying pan over a medium heat. Add the mushrooms and thyme and cook for about 7 minutes or until they are nice and coloured and the moisture they exude has been absorbed. Season, set aside and keep them warm.

Place a wide pan over a medium heat and add a few inches of water. Add the white wine vinegar and bring to a gentle simmer. Break an egg into a small cup and gently slide into the hot water. Repeat with three more eggs. Cook for 4 minutes, then carefully remove with a slotted spoon and place on absorbent kitchen paper.

Toast or grill the muffins or bread and place them on a warm plate. Divide the warm mushrooms evenly on top of each muffin or slice of bread and cover each with a poached egg. Pour a heaped tablespoon of hollandaise sauce over each egg and sprinkle with the lengths of chives.

New potato gratin with Reblochon cheese and wild mushrooms

Serves 6–8 (or more as an accompaniment)
Preparation time: 30 minutes, plus 1 hour 30 minutes
baking time

1 tablespoon olive oil, plus extra for greasing the dish
1 red onion, finely sliced
200 g/7 oz mixed wild mushrooms, cleaned and torn into
    even-sized pieces
2 large cloves garlic, finely chopped
400 ml/14 fl oz double cream
150 ml/5 fl oz milk
sea salt and freshly ground black pepper
900 g/2 lb large waxy potatoes, peeled and covered with
    water
250 g/8 oz Reblochon cheese, sliced

This extremely rich and creamy gratin is a hearty meal in itself. The cheese gives the dish a sweet nuttiness, while the wild mushrooms provide a deep earthiness. Try it with a simple salad, or serve smaller portions as an accompaniment to plain grilled meat or fish. Go easy on the portions, as it is quite filling.

Lightly brush a 20 x 30cm/8 x 12in roasting tin (or similar-sized gratin dish) with olive oil.

Place the tablespoon of olive oil into a large frying pan over a medium heat. Add the onions and cook for 2 minutes, then add the mushrooms and cook for a further 3 minutes. Add the garlic to the pan, stir to combine and cook for 1 minute. Transfer to a large mixing bowl and season well.

Preheat the oven to 150°C/300°F/gas mark 2. Mix the cream and milk together and season liberally, as the seasoning doesn't go far once it is mixed with the other ingredients.

Slice the potatoes very thinly, using a mandolin or a sharp knife, and add them to the mushrooms. Season well and stir to combine. Tip half the mixture into the roasting tin and lay half the cheese over the top. Add the remaining potato and mushroom mixture and pour the seasoned cream over. Place in the oven for 1 hour, then take out and top with the remaining cheese. Put back into the oven for a further 25–30 minutes or until the top is golden and bubbling. Remove the gratin from the oven and let it sit for 10 minutes before serving.

Steamed savoury custard with shiitake mushrooms and prawns

Makes 4 x 150 ml/5 fl oz custard cups
Preparation time: 30 minutes, plus about 12 minutes
for making the dashi

3 large eggs
2 teaspoons light soy sauce
1 teaspoons mirin*
300 ml/½ pint dashi stock (see miso soup recipe), cooled
4 medium shiitake mushrooms, tough stalks removed,
    sliced
4 large raw prawns, peeled and deveined
1 small spring onion (scallion), finely sliced

* mirin is a sweet sake available from Japanese grocers

These light and silky custards are traditionally served
as a small savoury accompaniment to Japanese meals,
but can also be served as a starter. For best results
the custards need to be cooked over a low heat to
prevent them bubbling. They should be cooked in a
bamboo steamer, which doesn't allow condensation
to gather in the lid.

Place a large bamboo steaming basket with a lid over a pan of
barely simmering water. Place the eggs, soy sauce and mirin
in a large bowl and whisk with a fork. Add the dashi stock,
stir to combine, and strain through a sieve into a jug. Set
aside to allow any air bubbles to disappear.

Place a quarter of the mushroom slices and one prawn into
each of the four small heatproof bowls or Oriental tea cups
(about 150 ml/5 oz capacity). Pour the egg mixture on top
of the mushrooms and prawns, leaving a 0.5 cm/¼ inch rim
at the top. Transfer the bowls or teacups into the steaming
basket and cover. Cook for 18 minutes, or until the custard
has just set but maintains quite a wobble. Gently remove the
cooked custards from the steaming basket, top each one with
some spring onion slices and serve piping hot.

Button mushrooms with white wine, olive oil and tomato

Serves 4–6 as a side dish
Preparation time: 30 minutes

3 tablespoons olive oil, plus extra for serving
150 ml/5 fl oz white wine
1 bay leaf
2 large sprigs oregano
1 teaspoon coriander seeds, crushed
1 tablespoon lemon juice
sea salt flakes and freshly ground black pepper
450 g/1 lb button mushrooms, cleaned and halved or
    quartered if large
2 medium ripe tomatoes
2 tablespoons chopped parsley

Place the oil, wine, bay leaf, oregano, coriander seeds and
lemon juice into a large non-reactive saucepan or sauté pan.
Season with ½ teaspoon of sea salt flakes and a generous
grinding of black pepper and place over a high heat. Stir to
combine and bring to the boil. Add the mushrooms, stir well,
and and lower the heat to a gentle simmer. Put the lid on the
pan and cook for 15 minutes, stirring every now and then.

Meanwhile, make a small cross with a sharp knife on the
base of each of the tomatoes. Put them in a bowl and cover
with boiling water, then leave for 30 seconds. Remove with a
slotted spoon and place in a bowl of cold water or under a
cold tap to cool them quickly. Once cooled, gently peel off
the skin, starting at the cross on the base; it should come
away easily. Quarter the tomatoes and deseed with a spoon or
knife. Chop the flesh and set aside until needed.

Remove the mushrooms from the pan with a slotted spoon
and place in a mixing bowl. Discard the bay leaf and oregano
stalks, then turn the heat up to high. Cook for 3 minutes, or
until the liquid has slightly reduced. Pour the liquid back
over the mushrooms, add the chopped tomatoes and stir
well. Taste and season if necessary. Allow to cool, then
transfer to a serving bowl, drizzle with some more olive oil
and top with the chopped parsley. Serve at room temperature.

Truffled wild mushrooms cooked in a foil parcel

Serves 4 as a starter, or 4–6 as an accompaniment
Preparation time: 40 minutes

60 g/2 oz butter, melted
300 g/10½ oz mixed wild mushrooms, cleaned and torn or
    cut into even-sized pieces
2 tablespoons chopped flat-leaf parsley
1 tablespoon chopped basil
2 teaspoons chopped tarragon
2 cloves garlic, finely chopped
sea salt and freshly ground black pepper
truffle oil, to serve

Be sure to serve this with lots of crusty bread to mop
up the fragrant garlicky juices.

Preheat the oven to 200°C/400°F/gas mark 6. Cut 2 large
squares of strong aluminium foil (with sides measuring
45 cm/18 in), place on top of each other and brush the
centre top sheet with melted butter, leaving a 10 cm/4 in
border. The measurements don't have to be exact, as long as
the sheets are big enough to hold the filling leaving enough
room to seal the edges.

Place the mushrooms in a large mixing bowl and add the
remaining butter, chopped herbs and garlic. Season well and
mix to combine. Tip the mixture into the middle of the
buttered section of foil. Bring the two long edges of foil
together over the mushrooms and fold or scrunch to seal,
making sure that the mixture is not too tightly packed in.
Fold the two shorter sides inwards, sealing them at the edges
to make a parcel. It should be well sealed but roomy inside,
as the mushrooms will cook in the steam they create.

Transfer the parcel to a baking sheet and place in the oven
for 20 minutes. Remove the parcel from the oven, open the
top, and place it on a plate. Drizzle over truffle oil to taste
and serve while steaming hot.

Warm brioche filled with morel mushroom scrambled eggs

Serves 2
Preparation time: 10 minutes, plus 20 minutes to soak
the mushrooms

10 g/⅓ oz dried morel mushrooms (about 5 medium ones)
2 small brioche
15 g/½ oz butter
3 large eggs
2 tablespoons double cream
sea salt and freshly ground black pepper

These velvety creamy eggs are made even richer
when paired with buttery brioche. Pure luxury!

Place the dried mushrooms in a small bowl, cover with warm
water for 20 minutes, and leave until softened. Squeeze the
mushrooms dry and finely slice, discarding the soaking water.

Preheat the oven to 150°C/300°F/gas mark 2. Cut off the
top third off each brioche and reserve – this will form the lid.
Using a teaspoon, and keeping the sides intact, scoop out the
middle of the brioche to create a well to hold the scrambled
eggs. Discard the bits that have been scooped out and place
the two bases and lids on a baking sheet. Place in the oven to
heat through while you prepare the scrambled eggs.

Place the butter in a non-stick frying pan over a low to
medium heat. Beat the eggs in a bowl and pour into the pan
with the sliced mushrooms. Cook for 3 minutes, stirring
continuously with a wooden spoon, until the mixture is
almost cooked - scrambled eggs carry on cooking in their
residual heat. Take off the heat and stir in the cream. Stir
well, taste and season.

Remove the brioche from the oven and place the 2 bases
on two warm plates. Fill each one with half of the creamy
eggs, top with the lids and serve immediately.

Spinach roulade with chanterelle mushrooms and smoked salmon

Serves 6 as a starter or light meal
Preparation time: 1 hour 15 minutes

For the spinach base:
500 g/1 lb spinach leaves
4 large eggs, separated
a few grindings of fresh nutmeg
sea salt and freshly ground black pepper

For the filling:
30 g/1 oz butter, plus extra for brushing the tin
250 g/8 oz chanterelle mushrooms, cleaned and torn
    into large pieces
2 tablespoons chopped chives
150 g/5 oz cream cheese
1 teaspoon lemon juice
freshly ground black pepper
150 g/5 oz oak-smoked salmon slices

This can easily be transformed into a tasty vegetarian dish by leaving out the salmon and replacing the cream cheese with a soft goat's cheese.

To make the spinach base, preheat the oven to 180°C/350°F/gas mark 4. Wash the spinach leaves in cold water and shake dry. Place a large saucepan over a medium high heat and add the spinach. Cook for 4–5 minutes, stirring often until the leaves wilt. Tip the softened spinach into a colander and rinse with cold water until cool. Squeeze dry several times, using your hands. Chop finely and place in a large mixing bowl. Add the egg yolks and nutmeg, season well and stir to combine. Lightly brush a 32 x 22 cm/13 x 9 in Swiss roll tin with butter and line with baking parchment.

Place the egg whites and a pinch of salt in a large mixing bowl and whisk until stiff, using an electric mixer. Spoon about a third of the whites into the bowl with the spinach and fold it in to loosen the mixture. Add the remaining whites and gently fold in until the mixture is incorporated. Pour into the prepared Swiss roll tin and place in the oven for 12 minutes or until cooked through. Allow to cool slightly, then gently turn out on to the middle of a clean tea towel.

To make the filling, place the butter in a large frying pan over a high heat. Add the mushrooms and cook them for 4 minutes, or until they soften and the excess liquid evaporates. Season well and transfer to a large plate to cool. Mix the chives, cream cheese and lemon juice together until smooth and season with pepper.

Position the spinach base and tea towel horizontally on a work surface. Smear the cream cheese mixture over the base, leaving a small gap along both of the long edges. Scatter the mushrooms over the cream cheese. Lay the salmon slices over the top and gently press down to compress the toppings. Using the long edge closest to you, roll the roulade up, working away from you up to the top edge until you have a thick cylinder. Gently transfer the roulade on to a long serving plate, with the seam facing downwards. When ready to serve, cut into 12 thick slices and eat with a lemon- and olive-oil-dressed salad.

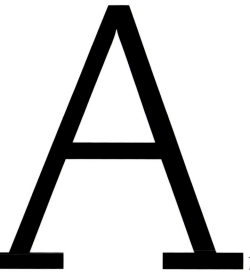lthough fine to store at home, fresh mushrooms are not supposed to hang around for too long as they become dry and chewy with age. Chilling mushrooms will prolong their storage life, and fresh unwashed mushrooms can be stored in the refrigerator for several days if handled correctly. Small amounts of mushrooms can be stored in loosely packed paper bags. Avoid plastic bags, however, as they tend to make mushrooms sweat. Mushrooms bruise easily if they are knocked about or poorly stored. Try to keep delicate mushrooms, especially the wild varieties, in a single layer to prevent them from getting bruised or squashed. If you are storing larger quantities of mushrooms, place them in shallow trays or containers and cover them with a tea towel to allow air to circulate around them.

Crispy potato cake filled with mixed mushrooms, sage and fontina cheese

Serves 4–6 as a light meal or 8 as a side dish
Preparation time: 1 hour 30 minutes

vegetable oil for shallow frying
large handful of sage leaves, plus 20 sage leaves, roughly
  chopped
900 g/2 lb medium-sized all-purpose potatoes
75 g/3 oz butter
1 large onion, very finely chopped
300 g/10 oz mixed mushrooms (wild and/or cultivated),
  cleaned and sliced
sea salt and freshly ground black pepper
150g/5 oz fontina cheese, thinly sliced

The fontina cheese can be substituted with any well-flavoured gooey melting cheese.

Place the oil in a frying pan set over a medium heat. Add the sage leaves, one by one, and cook until they are crispy. Remove with a slotted spoon and drain on some absorbent paper. Set aside in a dry place until needed.

Boil the whole unpeeled potatoes in a large pan of salted water for 15 minutes or until tender. Drain into a colander and set aside.

Meanwhile, place 15g/½ oz of butter in a 24 cm/10 in non-stick ovenproof frying pan over a medium to low heat. Add the chopped onion and cook for 5 minutes or until the onions soften. Transfer to a bowl and set aside. Wipe out the pan, put back on the heat, and add another 30 g/1 oz of butter followed by the mushrooms and chopped sage. It looks like a lot to fit in the pan but the mushrooms will soon shrink. Cook for 10 minutes, or until the mushrooms have softened and all of the moisture has been absorbed. Season, tip into a bowl, then wipe out the pan again and set aside. Preheat the oven to 200°C/400°F/gas mark 6.

Once the potatoes are cool enough to handle (but still hot), peel them with a peeler or small knife and roughly grate into a large mixing bowl. Add the softened onions, season and mix to combine.

Place the pan over a medium heat. Add 15 g/½ oz of butter, swirling it around until melted. Place half the potato mixture in the pan, squashing it down with a spatula, then top with the cooked mushrooms and the cheese slices. Spread the rest of the potato mixture over the top and push down lightly with wet hands, ensuring the mixture is compressed. Cook for 8–10 minutes, or until the base has browned. Transfer to a plate by placing the plate over the pan and carefully turning it upside down. Return the pan to the heat, add the remaining butter to the pan, swirl it around, and gently slide the potato cake back in, with the browned side facing up. Flatten again with a spatula and cook for 5 minutes. Transfer to the oven and bake for 20 minutes. Remove from the oven and loosen with a knife or spatula. Gently turn out on to a serving plate, scatter with the fried sage leaves and cut into wedges. Serve hot or warm.

Sausage, sage, crimini mushroom and chestnut stuffing balls

Makes 16 stuffing balls
Preparation time: 45 minutes

15 g/½ oz butter
3 shallots, finely chopped
150 g/5 oz crimini mushrooms, finely diced
45 g/1½ oz smoked bacon, thinly sliced
90 g/3 oz vacuum-packed chestnuts, roughly chopped
200 g/7 oz free-range pork sausages, skinned
30 g/1 oz fresh coarse breadcrumbs
1 heaped tablespoon finely chopped fresh sage
few grindings black pepper

These can be made ahead and chilled raw, then baked as needed.

Preheat the oven to 220°C/425°F/gas mark 7. Melt the butter in a frying pan over a medium heat and add the chopped shallots. Cook for 5 minutes, then add the mushrooms and cook for a further 5 minutes or until the mushrooms are soft. Transfer to a large bowl and allow to cool.

Add the remaining ingredients to the cooled mushroom mixture and mix well to combine. Roll into 16 balls, pressing firmly with your hands to compact the stuffing. Arrange the stuffing balls in a single layer on a lightly oiled baking sheet. Place in the oven for 12 minutes, then transfer to a warmed platter and serve.

Crimini mushrooms in spicy chickpea batter with mint raita

Makes 30
Preparation time: 25 minutes

for the mint raita:
150 ml/5 fl oz smooth natural yoghurt
1 teaspoon lime juice
1 tablespoon finely chopped mint leaves, plus extra for garnish
sea salt and cayenne pepper

175 g/6 oz chickpea flour*
½ teaspoon cayenne pepper
½ teaspoon ground cumin
½ teaspoon ground coriander
½ teaspoon salt, plus extra for seasoning
½ teaspoon bicarbonate of soda (baking soda)
200 ml/7 fl oz water
groundnut oil for deep-frying
30 crimini mushrooms, cleaned

* chickpea flour, also known as gram flour, is available from Indian grocers and some good health-food shops

Make the raita by stirring the ingredients together and seasoning to taste. Transfer to a small serving bowl and cover.

Make the chickpea batter by whisking together the chickpea flour, ground spices, salt, bicarbonate of soda and adding the water gradually until smooth.

Heat the oil in a deep-fryer. Place the mushrooms in the batter and toss to coat them well. Remove one mushroom with a fork, flick off any excess batter, repeating until you have enough for one batch. Place them in the fryer, cook for 2–3 minutes, then remove them with a slotted spoon and drain on some absorbent kitchen paper. Season with salt and place on a warm platter. Serve with the raita, topped with some extra chopped mint, and cook the remaining mushrooms, replenishing the platter as they are ready.

Shiitake mushroom, sesame and asparagus sushi rolls

Makes 3 long rolls (24 slices)
Preparation time: 1 hour 15 minutes

250 g/8 oz sushi rice*

3 tablespoons rice vinegar*

2 teaspoons sugar

½ teaspoon salt

6 asparagus spears

2 teaspoons groundnut oil

12 shiitake mushrooms, stalks discarded, caps thickly sliced

2 teaspoons mirin (sweet sake)*

2 teaspoons soy sauce, plus extra for serving

1 heaped teaspoon Japanese furikake seasoning** or toasted sesame seeds

3 sheets nori (dried seaweed sheets)*

wasabi (Japanese horseradish) paste*

* available from Japanese grocers
** furikake seasoning is a dry mix of seaweed, sesame and red shiso leaf available from Japanese grocers

Put the sushi rice into a heavy-based saucepan with 330ml cold water and bring to the boil. Once boiling, cover and reduce the heat to its lowest setting. Cook for 10 minutes, then turn off the heat and leave the pan covered for a further 15 minutes. You can prepare the rice seasoning, asparagus and mushrooms while the rice is cooking.

Make the rice seasoning by placing the rice vinegar, sugar and salt in a small pan over a low heat. Stir until the sugar dissolves, then take off the heat and allow to cool.

Snap the woody bases off the asparagus spears and discard. Place the spears in a pan of boiling water for 1½ minutes or until just cooked. Drain, then plunge them into a bowl of cold water to cool them down and allow them to retain their bright green colour. When cooled, place the asparagus on some absorbent kitchen paper and set aside until needed.

To make the seasoned mushrooms, place the oil in a frying pan over a medium heat. Add the mushrooms and cook for 2 minutes, tossing well to ensure that they brown evenly. Add the mirin and soy sauce and let the liquid almost bubble away. Transfer to a bowl, stir in the furikake seasoning or sesame seeds and allow to cool.

Once the rice is ready, tip it out into a wide shallow dish and sprinkle the seasoning on top. Begin to cool the rice by fanning it with a piece of cardboard or a paper fan. At the same time, use a long thin spatula to both help cool the rice and incorporate the seasoning by using cutting strokes and a gentle folding action. Be careful not to be too rough with the rice grains, as they are not supposed to be mashed. Continue moving and fanning the rice until it reaches room temperature.

Place a piece of nori, shiny side down, on a sushi rolling mat placed on a board. Moisten your hands with water and spread a third of the cooled rice over the nori, leaving a 2.5 cm/1 in gap along the edge furthest from you. If the rice starts to stick to your hands, just wet them a little more. Try to get the rice as flat and as even as you can. Place a dollop of wasabi paste on your finger and lightly smear it horizontally across the rice, about a third of the way up. Take a third of the cooled mushrooms and position them tightly across the line of wasabi. Take 2 spears of asparagus and position them base to spear across the length of the mushrooms (you may need to trim them for size). Using your fingers, moisten the exposed edge of nori with some water – this will seal the end of the sushi roll.

Using your fingers to compact the filling and your thumbs to roll, begin to roll the sushi mat from the edge closest to you. Press firmly as you go to create a tight roll. It should be nice and tight or it won't keep its shape once sliced. If it is too loose, simply unroll it and do it again. Keep rolling until you reach the moistened edge, then gently remove the mat and place the sushi roll seam side down on the board.

Dip a very sharp knife (the sushi won't cut neatly with a blunt knife edge) in water or wipe it with a wet cloth, and cut the sushi roll into eight even slices, moistening the knife between cuts to prevent the rice sticking. Place the rolls base down on a serving platter and hand round with a small bowl of soy sauce and a little extra of wasabi if desired.

Shiitake and hon-shimeji mushroom tempura with sweet mirin soy sauce

Makes 20 pieces
Preparation time: 20 minutes

For the dipping sauce:
1 tablespoon mirin*
1 tablespoon soy sauce
2 tablespoons water

groundnut oil for deep frying
180 ml/6 fl oz iced water
1 large egg yolk
90 g/3 oz plain flour
20 mushrooms - try small shiitake (stalks removed) or
    medium to large hon shimeji (separated)

* mirin is a sweet sake available from Japanese grocers

A light and crisp tempura batter is sublime, but quickly loses its appeal if it goes soggy. To ensure crispness, the water in the batter should be icy cold and the batter should be used as soon as it is prepared. If you are planning on making multiple batches of tempura it's best to make one quantity of batter at a time – it only takes a few seconds – so that each is always super-cold. Don't be alarmed by the lumpiness of the batter – it will look terrible, but if you resist the compulsion to smooth it out it will turn out fine. A final tip for crispness is to eat the tempura as soon as it's ready and serve it in a single layer so it doesn't go soggy.

Make the dipping sauce by placing all the ingredients in a small bowl and stirring to combine. Set aside while you prepare the tempura.

Heat the oil in a deep-fryer. Pour the iced water into a large bowl and add the egg yolk. Briefly stir with a chopstick or fork, then gently stir in the flour while still retaining some of the lumps. Tempura batter should be thin and lumpy, so it is important not to overwork the mixture by beating or whisking it.

Place a mushroom in the batter and slide it into the hot oil. Repeat with six or seven more mushrooms or as many as the pan will take without overcrowding. Cook for 1½ minutes or until the batter is lightly golden and crisp, turning the mushrooms over once during cooking. Remove from the oil and place on absorbent paper to drain. Transfer to a serving platter in one layer and serve immediately with the dipping sauce. Skim the oil to remove any bits of batter and repeat with the remaining mushrooms, serving each batch as soon as it is ready.

Chicken, shiitake mushroom and rice noodle spring rolls

Makes 20 mini spring rolls
Preparation time: 1 hour

for the filling:
5 dried shiitake mushrooms*
1 tablespoon groundnut oil
1 large clove garlic, finely chopped
1 teaspoon finely grated ginger
90 g/3 oz free range or organic minced chicken
30 g/1 oz white cabbage, finely sliced
15 g/½ oz carrot, cut into fine matchsticks
2 spring onions, finely sliced
2 teaspoons finely chopped coriander stalks, taken from the root end
2 tablespoons chopped coriander (cilantro) leaves and/or stalks
1 teaspoon sesame oil
1 tablespoon oyster sauce*
1 teaspoon cornflour (cornstarch) mixed with 1 tablespoon water
½ teaspoon sugar
⅛ teaspoon salt
large pinch ground white pepper
30 g/1 oz dried fine rice noodles*

for the spring rolls:
1 tablespoons plain flour
20 spring roll wrappers (13 cm/5 in squares)*
groundnut oil for deep-frying
sweet chilli sauce for dipping*

* available from Oriental grocers

These tasty party nibbles can be cooked the day before and heated in a warm oven when needed.

Reconstitute the mushrooms by placing them in a bowl of hot water for 20 minutes or until soft. Squeeze the mushrooms dry and remove the tough stems. Finely slice and set aside.

Pour the oil into a wok placed over a high heat. Add the chicken and cook for 1 minute. Add the garlic and ginger and cook for a few seconds, then add the mushrooms, cabbage, carrot, spring onion and coriander roots and leaves and cook for 2 minutes or until the vegetables begin to soften. Add the remaining ingredients, except the noodles, stir well and cook for a minute. Transfer to a mixing bowl and allow to cool.

Meanwhile, break up the dried noodles with your hands and place in a bowl. Cover with boiling water for 5 minutes or until the noodles soften. Drain in a colander, allow to cool slightly, then add to the cooled filling and mix well.

Mix the plain flour with 2 tablespoons water in a small bowl. This will be used to seal the spring rolls. Roll the spring rolls by placing a wrapper on a board with a corner pointing towards you. Place a tablespoon of the filling mixture across the bottom third of the wrapper. Fold the corner facing you upwards so it covers the filling and fold in the 2 sides to the edges. You will now have an envelope shaped top section. Brush this top corner with a small amount of the flour mixture and roll up tightly. Place on a tray and space out well.

Heat the oil in a deep-fryer and fry the spring rolls seven or eight at a time for 4 minutes, or until golden brown. Drain on absorbent kitchen paper, then place on a platter and serve with a small bowl of sweet chilli sauce.

Morel mushroom and pecorino tartlets with pistachios and pine nuts

Makes 20
Preparation time: 1 hour

20 g/⅔ oz dried morel mushrooms
30 g/1 oz butter, melted, plus extra for brushing
2 shallots, finely chopped
1 small clove garlic, finely chopped
4 tablespoons white wine
90 ml/3 fl oz double cream
30 g/1 oz pecorino cheese, finely grated
1 tablespoon pine nuts, toasted*
1 tablespoon chopped pistachio nuts*
1 tablespoon chopped chives
sea salt and freshly ground black pepper
4 sheets of filo pastry, each measuring 20 x 25cm/8 x 10in,
    kept covered until needed

* you can use just one type of nut and double the amount

Both the filling and the pastry cases can be prepared in advance, warmed through separately and assembled at the last minute. If you are really short of time you can buy the pastry cases, heat them up and simply fill them with the warm mushroom mixture.

Soften the mushrooms by soaking them in a bowl of warm water for 20 minutes. Squeeze the mushrooms dry and finely chop, discarding the mushroom water.

Place the butter into a small pan placed over a medium heat. Add the shallots and garlic and cook for 2 minutes or until they soften but don't colour. Add the chopped mushrooms and cook for a minute. Add the wine and cook for 1–2 minutes or until it evaporates. Add the cream and cheese and allow the mixture to thicken slightly. Take off the heat and stir in half each of the nuts and chives. Season and set aside until needed.

Preheat the oven to 190°C/375°F/gas mark 5. Lightly grease 20 bases of a 24-capacity mini-muffin tray. Place a sheet of filo pastry on a board and brush with melted butter. Lay a second sheet of pastry directly on top and brush with more melted butter. Press down to stick the sheets together, and cut the pastry into 20 squares each measuring 5 cm/2 in. A pizza cutter is ideal for this. Place two squares on top of each other at right angles to create a star. Repeat until you have 10 stars. Gently place the stars into the tin, pressing down to make a well for the filling. Repeat with the remaining pastry until you have 20 tartlet cases in total. Place in the oven and cook for 5 minutes or until the cases are golden brown.

Warm the filling through and distribute it evenly between the cooked pastry cases. Scatter the remaining nuts and chives over the top and serve on a warmed platter.

Portabellini mushrooms stuffed with pancetta, basil and pine nuts

Makes 12
Preparation time: 1 hour

12 small portabellini mushrooms, stalks removed
salt and freshly ground black pepper
1 tablespoon olive oil
1 onion, finely chopped
1 clove garlic, finely chopped
140 g/4½ oz pancetta, finely sliced or cubed
60 g/2 oz Parmesan cheese, grated
30 g/1 oz toasted pine nuts
2 tablespoons chopped basil leaves
2 tablespoons chopped flat-leaf parsley
60 g/2 oz fresh coarse breadcrumbs
1 egg, beaten

These stuffed mushrooms can be served as part of a buffet or eaten as finger food if you can get hold of smaller mushrooms. They also work well as a starter for four people.

Preheat the oven to 180°C/350°F/gas mark 4. Place the mushrooms, gill side up, on a lightly oiled baking tray and lightly season.

Pour the olive oil into a frying pan placed over a medium heat. Add the onion and cook for 3 minutes or until it begins to soften, then add the garlic and cook for a further minute or two. Add the pancetta and cook for 5 minutes. Take the pan off the heat, transfer to a mixing bowl and allow to cool.

Once cooled, add the cheese, pine nuts, herbs and breadcrumbs and season to taste. Add enough of the beaten egg to bind the mixture. Place 2 tablespoons of the stuffing on top of each mushroom, pressing down to compact the stuffing. Place in the oven for 20 minutes, then transfer to a serving platter and serve warm or hot.

Mixed mushroom, basil and Parmesan croquettes

Makes 16
Preparation time: 50 minutes

30 g/1 oz unsalted butter
3 shallots, finely chopped
450 g/15 oz mixed mushrooms, very finely diced
250 g/8 oz plain mashed potato, at room temperature
2 tablespoons chopped basil
30 g/1 oz Parmesan cheese, grated
salt and freshly ground black pepper
2 eggs
60 g/2 oz flour, seasoned with salt and freshly ground black pepper
90g/3 oz fresh coarse breadcrumbs
groundnut oil for deep-frying

Place the butter in a large frying pan over a medium heat. Add the shallots and cook for 2 minutes or until they are soft but not coloured. Add the mushrooms to the pan and cook for a further 5 minutes until they are dry and soft. Transfer to a large mixing bowl and set aside to cool.

Once cooled, add the potato, basil and Parmesan, stir to combine and season liberally. Divide the mixture into 16 balls (about 30 g/1 oz each) using wet hands, shape each into a little log and transfer to a large plate.

Beat the eggs in a wide shallow bowl. Place the flour on a large plate and the breadcrumbs on another. Place a croquette into the flour and toss to coat. Tap off any excess flour, then dip into the beaten egg and finally roll in the breadcrumbs until fully coated. Tap off any excess crumbs and place on a tray. Repeat with the rest of the croquettes.

Heat the oil in a deep-fryer and fry the croquettes in batches, five or six at a time, for 3–4 minutes or until golden brown. Transfer to a plate lined with kitchen paper and repeat with the remaining croquettes. Allow to cool for a few minutes, place on a platter and serve warm.

Rice paper rolls with enoki mushrooms and Chinese roasted duck

Makes 12 rolls
Preparation time: 40 minutes

½ Chinese barbecued duck, warm or at room temperature
12 small (about 15 cm/6 in) round rice papers*
24 coriander (cilantro) leaves
60 g/2 oz enoki mushrooms, separated
1 large spring onion (scallion), finely sliced
hoisin* or sweet chilli sauce*, to serve

* available from Oriental grocers

These rice paper rolls require no cooking, at least not on your part. Instead, leave it up to one of those Chinese restaurants that have beautifully lacquered roasted ducks hanging in the window. Just ask for a half duck and pick it apart at home.

Pull the meat and skin from the duck, discarding any fat. Shred or chop the meat and skin, and set aside.

Fill a wide shallow bowl with some warm water. Immerse a piece of rice paper in the water and repeat with another three, dropping in each one separately so they don't stick together. Leave for 1 minute or until softened, then gently lift each piece out and place them flat on a clean tea towel, without overlapping them. Place 2 coriander leaves in the middle of each circle. Lay a small pile of duck in a row across each circle, leaving a 2.5 cm/1 in gap on either side. Top the duck with some mushrooms and spring onions. Remember that the duck, mushrooms and spring onions have to make 12 rolls, so don't overdo it on the first few. Fold the bottom of the circle upwards to cover and tightly enclose the filling, then fold in the two vertical flaps to seal the sides. Roll up firmly, working your way up to the rounded edge on the top. Transfer to a serving platter. Cover with a damp cloth to stop them drying out, then repeat the process until you have 12 rolls. Serve with a small bowl of hoisin or sweet chilli sauce.

Wild mushroom vol-au-vents

Makes 20
Preparation time: 30 minutes

For the sauce base:
15 g/½ oz butter
1 level tablespoon plain flour
150 ml/5 fl oz milk, warmed
15 g/½ oz Parmesan cheese, grated
1 tablespoon pesto
2 tablespoons sour cream

15g/½oz butter
2 shallots, finely chopped
120g/4oz mixed wild mushrooms, cleaned and finely diced
sea salt and freshly ground black pepper
20 small cooked vol-au-vent cases
20 shavings Parmesan cheese

To make the sauce base, melt the butter in a small pan placed over a medium heat. Add the flour and stir or whisk to combine until smooth. Cook for 2 minutes, stirring a few times. Add a splash of the warm milk and whisk or stir until smooth. Gradually add the rest of the milk in small amounts, beating it smooth between additions. If you add too much milk at once the sauce can become lumpy. Cook for a few minutes, stirring often, until the sauce thickens. Take off the heat, stir in the Parmesan, pesto and sour cream, season well and set aside.

Preheat the oven to 180°C/350°F/gas mark 4. Place the butter in a non-stick frying pan over a medium heat. Add the shallots and cook for 3 minutes until softened but not coloured. Add the mushrooms and cook for a further 3 minutes, then take off the heat, season well and stir this mixture into the sauce.

Place the cooked vol-au-vent cases on a baking tray and fill each one with a scant tablespoon of the filling. Place in the oven for 6 minutes, or until the filling is warm. Transfer to a warmed serving plate, top each one with a shaving of Parmesan, and serve.

Porcini mushroom risotto balls filled with buffalo mozzarella

Makes 16 balls
Cooking time: 45 minutes, plus the time taken to cook the risotto

2 eggs, beaten
90 g/3 oz flour, seasoned with salt and freshly ground
    black pepper
90 g/3 oz fine dried breadcrumbs
750 g/1½ lb porcini mushroom risotto (see recipe,
    page 30) or any leftover mushroom risotto, cooled
125 g/4½ oz buffalo mozzarella, cut into 16 cubes
groundnut oil, for deep-frying

These crunchy oozing delights are known in their
native Italy as arancini, meaning 'little oranges'.
They can be handed round as party snacks, or can
serve 8 people as a starter when accompanied by
some lightly dressed salad leaves.
You should use a reasonably firm, cool risotto to make
these balls. If there is too much liquid in the risotto
they won't maintain their neat shape.

Beat the eggs in a wide shallow bowl. Place the flour on a
large plate and the breadcrumbs on another.

Wet your hands and place 45 g/1½ oz of cooled risotto in
your palm. Flatten to about 1 cm/½ inch thick and place a
mozzarella cube in the middle. Gently form into a tight ball
using both hands, making sure the cheese is fully enclosed.
Place on a tray and continue with the rest of the risotto.

Dip a risotto ball into the flour and toss to coat. Tap off
any excess flour, then dip into the beaten egg, then into the
breadcrumbs until fully coated. Tap off any excess crumbs
and place on a tray. Repeat with the rest of the balls.

Heat the oil in a deep-fryer and fry the balls, five or six at
a time, for 7 minutes or until golden brown. Transfer to a
plate lined with absorbent paper. Repeat with the remaining
batches. Place on a platter and serve hot or warm so the
cheese is still oozing in the middle.

Roasted portabello mushroom crostini with olive tapenade

Makes 24
Cooking   time: 40 minutes

24 thin slices baguette, sliced diagonally
4 tablespoons olive oil
180 g/6 oz portabello mushrooms (about 2 large ones)
6 large basil leaves, to serve

For the tapenade:
2 teaspoons small salted capers, rinsed to remove excess salt
1 small clove garlic, chopped
90 g/3 oz pitted green olives, chopped
6 large basil leaves, chopped
½ lemon
freshly ground black pepper

If you don't have a large mortar and pestle you can
make the tapenade in a small blender, or finely
hand-chop the ingredients and mix them together.

Preheat the oven to 180°C/350°F/gas mark 4. Place the
baguette slices on a baking tray and brush with a tablespoon
of the oil. Lightly season, place in the oven for 10 minutes or
until golden, then set aside to cool.

Place the mushrooms gill side up on a lightly oiled baking
tray. Drizzle with a tablespoon of olive oil, lightly season, and
place in the oven for 12 minutes or until cooked through.
Remove from the oven and set aside.

Meanwhile, make the tapenade by pounding the capers
and garlic together using a large mortar and pestle. Add the
olives and basil and grind to a rough paste. Add a squeeze or
two of lemon juice and season with pepper. It should not
need any salt, as the capers and olives are salty enough.

Roughly chop the cooked mushrooms into large chunks.
Place the crostini on a serving plate and top each one with a
spoonful of the tapenade. Lay the mushroom pieces over the
tapenade and drizzle with the remaining olive oil. Tear the
basil leaves, scatter them over the crostini and serve.

Oriental mushroom and ground pork san choy bow with crispy noodles

Makes 20 portions
Preparation time: 40 minutes

20 even-sized baby gem lettuce leaves, washed and dried
200 g/7 oz mixed oriental mushrooms (try shiitake,
    hon-shimeji, oyster and enoki)
groundnut oil for deep-frying, plus 2 extra tablespoons
30 g/1 oz dried fine rice noodles*
1 clove garlic, finely chopped
1 teaspoon finely shredded ginger
200 g/7 oz minced pork
8 tinned water chestnuts, roughly chopped
4 spring onions, finely sliced
2 tablespoons oyster sauce*
1 tablespoon hoisin sauce*
2 tablespoons water
½ teaspoon sugar
½ teaspoon sesame oil
handful fresh coriander (cilantro), roughly chopped
sweet chilli sauce, optional*

* available from Oriental grocers

These tasty lettuce cups can also be served as part of a meal for four by placing the filling into four large iceberg lettuce leaves, trimmed to form a neat cup shape. They can also be topped with a dollop of sweet chilli sauce if you like a little bit of spice.

Place the lettuce leaves in a bowl, cover with a damp cloth and refrigerate until needed. Remove the tough stalks from the shiitake mushrooms and finely slice. Roughly tear the oyster mushrooms and separate the other mushrooms from their clustered bases.

Heat the groundnut oil in a deep-fryer and loosen or lightly crush the noodles with your hands to break up the long lengths. Place about a third of the noodles into the hot oil until they puff up and turn white – this will only take a few seconds. Remove with a slotted spoon, place on some absorbent kitchen roll and repeat twice more with the remaining noodles. Set aside in a dry place.

Place a tablespoon of groundnut oil in a large wok or frying pan over a high heat. Add the garlic, ginger and pork and stir, cooking until the pork browns. Transfer the mixture to a bowl and place the pan back on the heat with another tablespoon of oil. Add the mushrooms and briskly fry until they are browned, then add the pork mixture. Add the water chestnuts, spring onions, oyster sauce, hoisin sauce, water and sugar and cook for a further minute. Remove from the heat and stir in the sesame oil and half the chopped coriander. Break all but a handful of the crispy noodles into the mixture, stir well and allow everything to cool slightly before assembling.

When you are ready to serve, place a heaped tablespoon of the mushroom mixture into each lettuce leaf. Top with a small dollop of sweet chilli sauce, if using. Place them on a large platter, scatter over the remaining coriander leaves and top each with a few crispy noodles.

Index

First published in 2004 by Conran Octopus Limited,
a part of Octopus Publishing Group,
2–4 Heron Quays, London E14 4JP
www.conran-octopus.co.uk

Publishing Director: Lorraine Dickey
Senior Editor: Katey Day
Assistant Editor: Sybella Marlow
Art Director: Chi Lam
Design: Victoria Burley
Production Manager: Angela Couchman
Photography: Tara Fisher
Prop Stylist: Róisín Neild
Home Economy: Jacque Malouf

British Cataloguing-in-Publication Data. ·
A catalogue record for this book is available from the
British Library.

ISBN 1 84091 405 X

To order please ring Conran Octopus Direct
on 01903 828503

Printed and bound in China

Author's Acknowledgements

Thank you…
Tara for beautiful images and unending (almost) patience
Katey for your trust and encouragement
Chi, Victoria and Carl for your creative talents
Róisín for truly covetable props
Tane for tasting, councelling and chauffering
May for being a multi skilled champion
Lynnie for schlepping to the markets in the dark
Harry for Friday aprons and assisting with enthusiasm
Henry for shooting the pheasants
(and Trouble for retrieving them)
Phil and the guys at the Mushroom Man for your fine produce
Le Creuset for your fabulous pots and pans